CW00972950

Fire from Heaven

Dawn of a Golden Age

Kiara Windrider

Fire from Heaven

Dawn of a Golden Age

First Edition, April 2005

www.kiarawindrider.com

Cover design by
Daniel B. Holeman
www.AwakenVisions.com

Text layout and design by K.R. Mohan Kumar

Co-Published by
Sai Towers Publishing
#23/1142, VL Colony, Kadugudi, Bangalore 560 067
tel: +91-(0)80-2845 1648, fax: +91-(0)80-2845 1649
www.saitowers.com

A catalogue record for this book is available from the British Library.

Typeset in 11 point Maiandra GD

ISBN 81-7899-050-4

Printed and bound in India by Vishruti Prints

Table of Contents

Part 2

Other Experiences of Enlightenment

Part 3

Collective Journey of Enlightenment

Part 4

Appendices

Foreword

By Members of The Golden Age Foundation

If you have ever wondered about what happened to the mystics of yore, this book is the answer. This book is a story of a man like you and me, who was taken to where we all want to be.

When Kiara was with us at the Oneness University, his insatiable thirst for wisdom and the humility to learn from everyone made him stand apart even in a crowd. His unique life experience and his multi-faceted cultural background make him the chosen author of this book.

Kiara has expressed his inner most thoughts in this book with utter simplicity and stunning authenticity. His book inspires the reader to the possibility of their own enlightenment without frightening them; as would the austere and trial filled path of the great sages and saints. He sends out his clarion call to all humanity announcing the incredible phenomenon of Amma and Bhagavan, bestowing the state of Oneness to all those who seek.

It brings to light the truth of Bhagavan's statement: *man cannot make it on his own; it has to be given to him.* Given it was to Kiara.

The book also is a treasure trove of some of the insightful teachings of Sri Bhagavan to the seeker. It will leave every reader astounded at the phenomenon of the divine grace of Amma and Bhagavan at work, landing man with effortless ease into the cherished state of Oneness. A journey that would otherwise take several life times and much travail, happening with such speed and ease in a such short period, leaves one wondering at the sheer magic of the *Deekshas*. Kiara's narrative is a testimony to this phenomenon.

When the book was read out, Sri Bhagavan remarked that the book itself could serve as a Deeksha to those who go through it. This book does not require application. It shows to you the futility of effort and awakens you to the power of God.

ꟹ

Preface

By Barry Martin

Somewhere in our hearts and souls we all know that God/ One/All That Is only wants us to be happy, abundant and joyful. Yet virtually all of us experience being prodigal sons and daughters roaming in the painful wastelands of suffering and limitation, creating more of the same for ourselves and the Earth. Despite all of our efforts, most of us seem unable to find our way back to the 'kingdom of heaven' – our natural awakened state. Yet the Divine is always providing avenues for us to find our way home.

A most profound doorway back to our native state of enlightenment has descended in the form of Bhagavan, an avatar of enlightenment living outside a small town in southern India. Through a series of synchronicities, I was called to his abode in February, 2004. There, I was blessed with the most profound experiences of this life. And I saw hundreds of people experience the profound grace of the Divine. They were awakened, easily and spontaneously, to the truth of their being: oneness, joy, happiness and bliss. The end of the long road back to the true Self, or no self, which often entails a lifetime of practices and disciplines, was reached so easily and effortlessly that it was at once unfathomable and yet totally natural.

The fire of the possibility of a mass collective awakening burned brightly as I returned to the West. For decades I had felt sure a collective awakening was imminent, yet my mind puzzled over exactly how it would happen, since it knew of no earthly presence or vehicle capable of facilitating such an awakening on a massive scale.

Now, after the experiences at Bhagavan's abode, I knew, beyond all doubt, that the collective awakening was underway! I also saw that it could culminate in an awakened planet in the very near future, within the next few years. Since my own re-awakening, in my mind's eye I see humanity as already awakened – not as a possibility, but as a reality, beyond time and space.

After the trip to India, I found myself telling friends how absolutely natural it was to return to the enlightened state. Most seemed unable to completely open their hearts and minds to the possibility that, through grace, they could be awakened so quickly and easily. The collective separated mind contains many distorted images and concepts about what enlightenment is, along with cynicism, disbelief, and a deep unconscious sense of unworthiness. The separated self sense not only resists the possibility of enlightenment, but actually defends against it, knowing that awakening will end its illusory existence.

All that we believe about enlightenment, and all that we do to try to bring about this state, arise from the very sense of separate self that must surrender and 'die' for grace to descend and enlightenment to occur. Yes, we can prepare ourselves; our efforts are not in vain. But, in the end, it is only through total surrender that enlightenment can occur.

Divine grace through Bhagavan is calling many to come home to their natural, joyous state of being.

This book is one of the avenues through which the transmission of this grace is moving across the face of the planet. That you now hold it in your hands is no coincidence. Bhagavan has said that in order to take the next step we must be willing to admit that we are suffering, and we must sincerely desire to go beyond suffering. He adds that we need to admit that all of our efforts have not resulted in attaining enlightenment. Finally, we must be willing to surrender to grace and divine assistance, in whatever forms they come.

For many, Kiara's book will prove to be one of those forms. I encourage those who find themselves called to this book to refrain from 'reading' it. Instead, I suggest entering into a process of deeply considering what you find here. To 'read' is to enter the labyrinth of the limiting, veiling, and obscuring filters of the collective human mind field. Only bits and fragments of truth can be found within the maze of the separated ego mind. In contrast, when we choose to deeply consider what we find here, we invite the essence of the book into the realms of heart and soul. As we relax into a childlike state of openness and willingness, the transmission of the divine that informs Kiara's writing can catalyze a journey of awakening and illumination.

Fire from Heaven is a gift of grace to assist humanity in returning to the natural state of enlightenment. More than a collection of concepts and ideas, the book is a vessel for the awakening grace itself, an inculcation of the frequencies of enlightenment. May it be your doorway to the Home you have always sought!

Introduction

What do you say after the search of lifetimes has ended?

For me, as for many people, enlightenment had always been a destination at the end of the road. Whenever someone asked me to define my highest goal in life, I always said, "Enlightenment". I could never see beyond that. I was so attached to the seeking, the questing, the journeying, what was there to do with my life afterwards? Who would I be if I ever stopped seeking?

No wonder it took so long! While I craved enlightenment, some part of me also resisted it. Enlightenment is a warrior's path, I realize now. You search, you struggle, you fight to get there. And when you finally do, you're dead!

Who dies? After enlightenment I realized it is only the 'self' which dies - the little fixated self, also known as the 'ego' – which was forever seeking, urging, comparing, judging, never allowing itself to be still because it was afraid that somehow life would pass by with nothing to show for it.

What did I know of life before? Even though I had been on a spiritual path for a long time, I had still very much been identified with one little fixation in the boundless flow of life that I called 'me' - the me that felt so unworthy sometimes, and was always yearning for more, the self that felt so powerless and was always holding on to what it knew, the self that felt so small it had to force the universe to fit into its own little concepts of it.

This little 'me' had tried so desperately to control everything in my life! Yet, what did I know of the brilliance of life, the endlessly creative rhythms of the universe that were constantly beating through my heartbeat in every moment of existence? In constantly trying to control my life I had only succeeded in separating myself from the river that was constantly seeking to carry me home.

How did I come to the end of the search? Near a small village in south India, in a place known as Oneness University, there is an avatar named Bhagavan (not to be confused with Osho, who was also referred to as Bhagavan). People call him a 'mukti avatar', and his life mission is to give enlightenment to the world. He says that enlightenment is a neurobiological process, and that all it takes is a little adjustment in the brain, which then allows the cosmic energies to flow through and dissolve the concept that we carry around of a separately existing 'self', which is in fact only an illusion of perception.

This happens through a process known as the 'deeksha', a transfer of divine energy in which someone who is so trained can place their hands on your head and allow cosmic energies to channel through. This energy is programmed to lead to enlightenment. Many people experience a golden ball descending into their heads, and a restructuring of the brain begins to take place.

As this restructuring continues to happen, people begin to enter into deep states of silence, peace, joy, or cosmic consciousness. At a certain point, they discover that there is no more a reference point called the 'self'. All that remains is the vast ocean of consciousness. The drop dissolves into the ocean, or perhaps, the ocean dissolves into the drop. All concepts about reality and spirituality dissolve into the direct experience of it.

This book not only describes my own journey of enlightenment, and that of a few others who are well known to me, but also holds out the possibility of a planetary enlightenment. There are thousands who have received this state here at Bhagavan's abode, and his mission is ultimately to give enlightenment to every human being on this planet.

What Bhagavan gives is not a watered down version of enlightenment, but the same consciousness experienced by a Buddha, a Christ, or a Ramana Maharshi. It is not based on teachings, morality, or effort, but a gift of grace transferred through a process known as the 'deeksha', which initiates a shift in the neural circuitries of the brain, leading to enlightenment. Enlightenment is a neuro-biological event, insists Bhagavan. Once enlightened, however, it is also a continually deepening process.

There are so many teachings in the world today, so many traditions and practices, but as many seekers have discovered, these in themselves are not enough to produce enlightenment. Yet, as gift of grace transferred through the deeksha, enlightenment can happen to the simple villager as easily as to the most ardent spiritual seeker, perhaps easier, since he is not bogged down by so many expectations and concepts. It is our natural state, Bhagavan insists.

Bhagavan has never said that his is the only way to get enlightened, and has little interest in telling people what they should do or not do. He has no interest in creating yet another religion. His sole mission is to facilitate enlightenment for everyone whose souls desire this.

He often refers to himself as a 'technician', as one who is capable of creating certain neurobiological shifts in the brain in order to produce enlightenment. It is a 'divine operation', and has nothing to do with dogma, belief, or rituals. Although physical proximity can help, this transmission is beyond the limitations of space and time.

Bhagavan's teachings are universal. "I belong to the whole world and all the world's faiths", he asserts. He emphasizes that all religions have their own purpose, and there is no need for conflict between them. He also emphasizes that enlightenment has nothing to do with religion. Once we become enlightened our guiding light comes directly from within. Once we become spiritually mature we will not need external moral codes to adhere to. He predicts that organized religions will die a natural death after global enlightenment is accomplished.

My intention in this book is to share Bhagavan's teachings as simply as possible, without using too many metaphysical concepts, so that it can be relevant to every seeker, and even to those who might consider themselves beyond religious teachings. Ultimately, the only purpose of these teachings is to point out what you already know, and to guide you into the experience itself.

As I share my own experience of receiving enlightenment, it is with the absolute conviction that anybody is capable of receiving this gift as well. Ultimately, as more and more people become enlightened, the ripples of enlightenment will sweep through the entire planet, whether they are on a spiritual path or not, and even whether they believe in the possibility or not. It is our divine destiny, says Bhagavan.

Something is changing in the consciousness of humanity. We entered the long-awaited Golden Age in 2003 AD, says Bhagavan, and a new biological species with new genetic possibilities is consequently emerging that will be 'wired' to the state of Oneness.

As such, the enlightenment spoken about in this book will soon become a normal way of being for everyone on Earth, and indeed there are many today who are already experiencing spontaneous awakenings. For those who would like assistance, however, the deeksha programs are being offered at Oneness University, and also around the world, by people who have undergone the training to transmit this state.

Indeed, after reading the manuscript for this book, Bhagavan affirmed that these pages themselves could serve as a deeksha. Bhagavan's energy was very strongly present in the writing of this book, and will likewise be with you as you read through these pages. Most of this book was written in a 10 day period of time, when his energy came through in a flow of inspiration so strong that I could not humanly stop writing. As I share these experiences, it is my wish that all who read this book may be similarly blessed, knowing that the time of your soul's deepest fulfillment is now here.

In the final chapter of this book, I share briefly Sri Aurobindo's vision of the 'supramental descent'. My hope is to provide a larger context for the amazing revolution that is now taking place in human evolution, in which Bhagavan is playing such a key role. At the very end, is a conversation with Bhagavan himself, followed by an appendix highlighting various perspectives on the upcoming 'shift of the ages' summarized from my earlier book, *Doorway to Eternity: A Guide to Planetary Ascension.* I believe this will be relevant to readers who wish to understand the scientific as well as mystical basis for our planetary transition into the 'golden age'.

Two more appendixes, written in conversation with neuro-scientist, Christian Opitz, highlight the relationship between enlightenment, deeksha, and the brain from a neuro-biological perspective. Since some of the spiritual terms used throughout this book may be unfamiliar to some readers, I am also including a glossary at the back of the book.

We are entering an age, whether we call it the Golden Age or Satya Yuga or the Aquarian Age, or the Fifth World, where the veils between the spiritual and material worlds are actually beginning to dissolve. There once was a time when we were born enlightened, and lived in constant awareness of the unity of all things. In the course of time, for reasons that philosophers and theologians can argue endlessly about and don't really matter anymore, we chose to create a dense veil between various aspects of ourselves. These veils are held in our subconscious memory as patterns of separation, forgetfulness, limitation, illusion, fear, and so on.

Our genes mutated to align with these subconscious patterns. This in turn created pathways within our brain which generated the illusion of a 'self' that existed separate from everything else. When the deeksha is given these pathways dissolve, and we begin to experience reality from the perspective of oneness. When enough people experience this shift in perspective, a 'critical mass' will be reached, affecting the collective DNA of humanity. Once this critical mass is reached, global enlightenment will happen.

"When the last trumpet sounds," says the Book of Revelations, "we will be changed in the twinkling of an eye." Well, the last trumpet has sounded, and the presence of beings like Bhagavan in the world today reflects the deep human thirst to break out of illusion, to unplug from the 'matrix', and to reconnect with our divine blueprint.

We cannot solve humanity's problems from the same level of consciousness in which they were created. But we can enter a collective state where the problems themselves disappear in the light of an awakened consciousness. This is happening now.

It is an exciting time to be alive. Given what I know today, there is no place I would rather be in this entire vast cosmos than right here on Earth during this glorious time of awakening. We have waited eons and lifetimes for this, and I echo, along with Bhagavan, that despite all the evidence of my outer senses, there is no doubt in my mind or heart that humanity is going to make it!

The entire world is but a dream in the mind of God. This book is the story of this Dream, and of humanity's awakening within the dream!

~~~~~~~~~~ ✹ ~~~~~~~~~~

Brother Sun

Brother sun, I asked one day,
Don't you ever tire
Of spinning endless circles across the sky?
Rising, then setting,
Eternal mystery of day and night?
He looked at me then,
Gazing softly into my heart,
Filling me deep with his light.
It is not I that spins through the skies
Creating days and nights, he said.
Here there is only undying light
Of eternal radiance;
All else is your perception.
See me and you shall see yourself;
All shadows are lifted
In noonday light.
Once you have seen,
No longer can you be a little speck
That blows around
Like chaff in the wind,
Separate and alone.
You too shall become a sun
Of undying light;
Yes, be a sun unto yourself,
And we shall circle,
Always eternally within each other.

~~~~~~~~~~ ✹ ~~~~~~~~~~

Part I

My Journey of Enlightenment

1. The Search

There is nothing like being on a journey towards a far land, not knowing the way, not sure the destination exists, somehow knowing I am destined to arrive to God, yet aware also that the self that finally arrives is equally destined to disappear. What can I say about this journey, except to affirm that it only begins after it is over? What can I say about the self, except to know that I only understand myself when 'I' am gone? What can I say about discovering God, except to marvel at all the continually changing infinitely beautiful expressions of God's face, which is also my own face?

Ever since I can remember I have been fascinated by stories of holy men and women in the mountaintops and forests of

India living in enlightened states of divine union. Yogananda Paramahamsa's '*Autobiography of a Yogi*' was a firm favorite, along with Swami Rama's '*Living with the Himalayan Masters*'.

I looked to the extraordinary beings filling these pages with admiration and some envy, recognizing the longing deep in my heart to achieve a similar state of enlightenment, yet convinced I did not have the discipline nor stamina required to spend years in a cave hidden away from the world seeking this most precious of all pearls.

Over the years I gave up hope. I would never be a Buddha or a Christ or a Ramana Maharshi, for those were the only images I had of what an enlightened person looked like. I would escape into fantasies of becoming enlightened, not just as a personal experience but as a global awakening, but I always managed to find my way back to 'reality', a word I didn't particularly like, because it had nothing to do with what felt real, yet was something I had to learn to deal with if I were to be of any use on Earth.

I justified the abandonment of my quest. How could I feel good about entering into some kind of personal nirvana while billions of earthlings were hell-bent on extinction? How could I justify spending years in a solitary cave when the voices of human need were so loud all around me? What kind of answers made sense in a world where outer reality seemed to be dominated by greed, hunger, manipulation, destruction, and suffering? Besides, I had been told that only a handful of people had achieved this state since the dawn of history, so what chance did I have of being next in line?

Still, the longing in my heart remained, and I tortured myself with the yearning to break free from the limitations I perceived within my own experience of self, all the while knowing that this was an impossible dream. I was not an avatar, I was too lazy and undisciplined to even meditate regularly, so what was I doing on this quixotic quest? "To dream the impossible dream, to fight the unbeatable foe, to bear with unbearable sorrow, to run where the brave dare not go". These words from Don Quixote's quest were mine as well. The longings fed the faraway hope that someday somehow I would make it, making the emptiness of the moment a little more bearable.

My journey is not so different from that of anyone else, for underneath all of our separate illusions of reality, there is essentially one soul, one mind, one body, and one consciousness. As I share this journey of awakening, you will perhaps see that it is your journey as well. And more than that, it is also the journey of the vast unified consciousness that is the collective consciousness of this planet.

I begin my story with an incident which jolted me out of my complacency one beautiful sunny morning when I was 16. I was a student at the Kodai International School in the lushly forested hills of south India. One fine weekend, a group of us were out on one of our favorite hikes along a beautiful winding mountain stream that led to a steeply cascading waterfall that dropped hundreds of feet into a gorge below.

We camped overnight near the stream, and after a quick breakfast the following morning, two of us went ahead of the group down to the waterfalls. Somewhat intoxicated by the perfection of the beauty all around us, we decided to climb down the falls as far as we could. We had climbed several hundred feet when my friend lost his hold and fell. I watched him fall in petrified shock, and continued to watch in frozen horror as I lost my own grip and started to fall.

Fingernails torn and bloody from trying to stop myself, I bounced rapidly down the steep cliffside, realizing that there was nothing more I could do. Soon, I found myself surrendering to the inevitability of death, and strangely enough, a great peace washed over me. I entered a time zone where everything seemed to slow down, and in my next moment of conscious awareness I found myself standing in a pool, waist deep in water on a ledge of rock jutting out from the cliff, with hundreds of feet of cascading water still below us. Amazingly, my friend had also landed in the same pool. We had fallen 200 feet, and although hurt and dazed, we were inexplicably, gloriously, alive! I realized then that there was a purpose to my life, and that I had been kept alive to fulfill that purpose.

In the months and years afterwards I embarked on a fervent quest to understand the meaning and purpose of my life. I studied and explored the teachings and practices of just about every world religious tradition that existed. After graduating from high school I spent several years living and studying in various ashrams in India – Hindu, Buddhist and Christian.

There came a point when I intentionally gave up all organized religion, realizing that much of it was too imbedded in the past, and feeling like I needed to find a path that spoke more directly to our contemporary human condition, while at the same time being deeply connected with the Source of all things.

When I was 21, I received a scholarship for a college in the USA. Bethel College is a small college in Kansas, deeply grounded in the Mennonite traditions of peace and justice. Inspired by people like Gandhi and Martin Luther King, I became increasingly aware of the political dimensions of Jesus' ministry.

I began to realize that my spirituality had to extend into the marketplace, engaging with the political, social and economic realities of the world around me, changing not just individuals but also systems, in order to affect not only their spiritual, but also their physical realities. I majored in Peace Studies and International Development, and spent some years actively involved within the peace and environmental movements, struggling to create a better world through political activism.

Ever since I was young I had been passionately interested in saving the environment, and in researching alternative, earth-friendly technologies. I had always felt deeply distressed by humanity's blindness and greed towards nature, and couldn't even bear to see a tree being cut down. During my years in college I connected with the Native American path, a path representing oneness with nature, and with the Great Spirit.

I became interested in shamanism, in understanding the spirit that moved through all things, and in speaking directly with Great Spirit through nature and through what the Australian aborigines called the Dreamtime. I yearned to develop the mystical connection with trees, animals, and nature spirits that the indigenous people all over the world seemed to still maintain. Over the years this led me to learn what amounted to a form of "channeling", where I began to attune to the consciousness of nature spirits, angels, ascended masters, and cosmic beings.

During this time I also become fascinated by the insights of quantum mechanics, astrophysics, and biology, exploring the nature of the universe and the evolution of consciousness. My father is a physicist, and so I've always had an interest in the natural sciences, but here I was beginning to walk the bridge between science and spirituality, and it was exciting to see the underlying unity between them. Each spoke a different language, but pointed to the same reality, ultimately a reality that could not be easily understood except through direct intuitive experience.

I had also become very interested in the relationship between soul, brain, and consciousness. Many enlightened people, such as UG Krishnamurthy and Gopi Krishna, were emphasizing that their enlightenment was not a spiritual event but a biological one, related to an evolutionary shift in the chemistry of the brain, and this intrigued me. I also began to study what scientists such as Dr. Valerie Hunt were saying about the neuro-biology of enlightenment, and became very interested in technologies that could help in changing brain states.

The thirst for direct experience eventually led me back to school. At one of the ashrams where I had lived in India, I became interested in the works of Ken Wilber, Stan Grof, and other leaders in the field of transpersonal psychology, which sought to unify the best of spirituality and psychology in the quest to live out the ultimate in human potential. One of the techniques I learned was Holotropic Breathwork, combining intensive breathing with music designed to activate each of the seven chakras in the human energy system.

I practiced this for a period of time, which activated some intense realizations in my psycho-energetic being. I realized that I wanted to spend my life helping people achieving similar states, and so in my mid-twenties found myself enrolled in a graduate program called the California Institute for Integral Studies, founded by a disciple of the great Indian yogi, Sri Aurobindo. Five years later, I graduated from John F Kennedy University with a degree in Transpersonal Counseling Psychology.

Along with my graduate program I was forever taking all kinds of workshops, learning various forms of therapeutic massage and bodywork, doing Enlightenment Intensives and Vipassana retreats, exploring various channeled teachings, interacting with various spiritual teachers, doing Sweat Lodges, participating in Sufi Dancing, and generally exploring every form of spiritual teaching to be found under the California sun.

Shortly after I enrolled at the California Institute for Integral Studies, I began to feel a kind of dissolution of the self, as if my subtle bodies were coming into a vast state of union with a Himalayan Master that I had been connecting with who was known simply as Babaji. For many months I felt that my own sense of identity had dissolved, and I would wake every morning with strong currents of energy coursing through my body. I experienced a state of bliss, accompanied by many realizations about the nature of the universe and human consciousness. After a few months, however, this state faded and eventually disappeared, leaving me with a profound sense of disappointment and failure.

After graduating, I worked for some years as a psychotherapist at an alternative healing center known as the Pocket Ranch Institute. It was directed by Barbara Findeisen and Tony Madrid, whose dream was to provide a safe place for people to go through spiritual crisis and kundalini awakening.

Affiliated with the Spiritual Emergence Network, we had various programs for people to release emotional traumas from the past, and to reconnect with their higher selves. The ranch was situated in 3000 acres of wild oaks, mountain streams and open meadows, on land that had been held sacred as a place of spiritual visioning for hundreds of years. It was a unique program, and I loved every minute of it.

My home during this time was in Mount Shasta in California, considered by many to be one of the most powerful vortexes of sacred energy on the planet. I spent a lot of time up in the alpine meadows, communing with the spirits of the mountain, and with the ascended masters whose presence is so tangible there. It was a beautiful time of discovery, broadening my vision of what our planetary journey was all about. I also spent a lot of time in Hawaii, playing with the dolphins and whales in their ocean world, allowing them to teach me about oneness.

Gradually, I started putting various pieces together that seemed to point to a world of new possibilities. I studied various calendar systems and prophecies from around the world, I researched little-known scientific findings that pointed to huge shifts in consciousness coming our way, I found myself inspired by future visions that people were having all over the world, and even found myself 'channeling' aspects of myself from other timelines, all of which pointed towards a collective shift that awaited humanity in the near future. I wrote a book about all this, '*Doorway to Eternity: A Guide to Planetary Ascension*', which immediately won a number of awards, and glowing commendation from a number of people who were beginning to come to the same conclusions.

What was missing, however, was a plan. It was all very well to say that this is where humanity was headed, and even to feel the truth of this on a very deep level. Still, I felt somewhat schizophrenic sometimes when I would read about another round of terrorism in yet another corner of the Earth, whether state-sponsored or otherwise, or hear about another tribe of indigenous people displaced as their forest was destroyed so that yet another corporate entity could profit from the blood of the living Earth.

Was there a point of convergence between my deeply felt inner visions and these deeply fractured outer realities? Or was I simply becoming another casualty of a 'head in the clouds' spirituality that was no longer relevant to the outer world?

2. Meeting Bhagavan

In early 2002 I met a woman who later became my wife. Her name was Grace. Shortly after we met she had a vision where an ancient being appeared to her in the guise of an Indian woman draped completely in plain white cotton. She revealed herself to be 'Mother India', and showed her a vast landscape that lay dry and barren under a waterless sky, with deep cracks in the ground several inches wide. Only a few people wandered in the distance.

"My children are dying", she said. "They need food, they need water, they need people who care. People must begin to care". Grace remained in that waking vision for an entire day, deeply feeling the pain, parched with heat and thirst, and throwing up repeatedly. She became vast. She was Mother India, and felt her body had become the land. She felt like she was vomiting up earthquakes for India so they wouldn't have to be experienced by the land physically.

Inexplicably, after 22 years of having lived in the US, I too began feeling a strong urge to return to the land of my birth, India. As I spoke about this with a trusted friend, Barry, he had the premonition that I would meet somebody who could guide me into the highest states of enlightenment, something we had both been seeking for a long time. I deeply resonated with his statement, and felt the truth of it as a deep upwelling of joy throughout my body.

Neither of us knew why or where, but both Grace and I knew we had to go. The call was becoming too strong to ignore. We packed up our bags, put everything into storage, and were on a plane to India by late September.

We traveled through many ashrams, met many yogis and gurus. We became attracted to the works of Sri Aurobindo, a freedom fighter, mystic, and highly accomplished yogi who had lived much of his life in deep contemplation in Pondicherry, India. Joined in this work later by a Frenchwoman, Mirra Alfassa, who eventually came to be known as the Mother, his great task was to anchor into the collective consciousness of humanity what he referred to as the 'supramental force', a force that he claimed would most surely awaken humanity into her true evolutionary destiny as a supramental species, as far beyond the current human species as humanity is beyond those who have preceded us.

Grace and I spent much time in Auroville, the city of human unity founded by the Mother after the death of Sri Aurobindo. We connected deeply with the spirit of these two visionaries, and had some powerful glimpses of the supramental realms. We spent a lot of time meditating in the Matrimandir, a golden sphere in the center of Auroville, which represented a vehicle for the descent of this supramental force.

One day, as we were meditating in the early dawn, Grace had a visitation from a beautiful, tall, male being, smeared in ash, greenish-grey in color, bare-chested, hair up in a topknot, and then down in dreadlocks. He had garlands of beads around his neck.

There was an aura of powerful benevolence about him. He extended his hand to her, holding out what appeared to be a long, luminous oval swirling with a soft green and pink opalescence. She heard the words "cosmic egg". He was so real she could touch him. She didn't know who he was, but as she described him to me I realized that this was Shiva. The image remained in her consciousness for weeks, and seemed to be a guiding force as we journeyed along.

In August 2003, we were guided to meet an avatar named Bhagavan. I had been invited to speak at The Experience Festival, a bi-annual event co-sponsored by his Golden Age Foundation, and the Global Oneness Foundation, brainchild of two Swedes, Jonas Lindquist and Parlan Fritz. Towards the end of this weeklong event, Grace and I, along with the other teachers at the event, were invited to have a darshan with Bhagavan.

'Bhagavan' literally means 'divine avatar', or 'bestower of blessings', and is a commonly used title in India to refer to someone who is God-realized. In his case, it is not a title, but his legal name as entered in the government records when certain spiritual phenomena first started happening around him. He had previously been known as Kalki, but is now firmly insisting that people not use that name anymore. It was creating too much controversy for too many people, since the term 'Kalki' also refers to the tenth incarnation of Vishnu, one who was promised in the Hindu scriptures to come at the end of the Kali Age to promote righteousness and heal the world.

In this context, Bhagavan acknowledges that if this is true for himself, it is also true for everybody else who feels that their mission is to bring healing and enlightenment to the planet. Just as the 'Second Coming of Christ' for many Christians refers not to a single person but to a collective force of unified consciousness, so is 'Kalki' a collective avataric presence. Anyone who is enlightened, and is working for the enlightenment of humanity, is a Kalki!

I also want to emphasize again here, especially for Western readers, that the 'Bhagavan' I speak about in this book is not synonymous with the well-known spiritual teacher, Osho, who was also referred to by the same title. In fact, 'Bhagavan' is a very common title used in India, except that in this case it is his legal name as well.

Bhagavan is an avatar, which can be defined as a descent of divine consciousness into humanity. Within the Hindu tradition an avatar manifests during a time when our spiritual development has stagnated, and when we need a form of divine intervention in order to move us forward.

There can be many kinds of avatars, and each avatar's role is very specific. Avatars can work on many levels of consciousness, which can be classified as either earthly or cosmic in nature. For example, Einstein was an avatar of physics, and Gandhi was an avatar of non-violence, while Jesus was an avatar of love, and Ramana Maharishi was an avatar of wisdom. Bhagavan's own special mission, along with that of his wife, Amma, is to be an avatar of enlightenment, a 'mukti avatar'. They are often considered as a single avataric consciousness in two bodies.

Meeting him was an unforgettable experience. We experienced Bhagavan as a warm, wise, pragmatic, and very transparent human being. When asked about what he does, he claimed to be able to transmit states of enlightenment through a process known as the 'deeksha'.

Enlightenment cannot be earned, he stated. If this were true, all the millions of spiritual seekers in every age should have been enlightened by now. It could be given, however. He referred to himself as a technician, and said it was possible to permanently enlighten the consciousness of the seeker by shifting the neurobiological structure of the brain. It was an astounding claim to make.

I watched my reactions to this statement. Having lived many years in the West, and always wary of being duped by yet another guru with something to sell, a red flag immediately went up in my mind. Isn't enlightenment something you had to earn for yourself, I wondered? How could someone give it to you? And wasn't it true, as I had come to rationalize after a lifetime of fruitless searching, that you are already enlightened, if only you pretend hard enough?

Still, we both felt a strong resonance with his words, and a deep excitement in our hearts. We happened to be at Amma's birthday darshan in Nemam when the first public deekshas were given, and immediately afterwards enrolled in a weeklong 'mukti' program and received a couple more deekshas. I watched Grace go through an amazing process of transformation resulting a few days later in her enlightenment.

We had both been on a spiritual path for a long time, and had steadfastly practiced all kinds of meditation practices, psychotherapies, healing techniques, and metaphysical teachings, but neither of us had ever experienced anything close to what was happening here. We knew in our hearts that this was the reason we had been led to come to India.

We had an opportunity to talk with Bhagavan after her enlightenment, and during that time I asked him why it was that I hadn't become enlightened as Grace had. He told me that he could give it to me immediately if I so chose, but that I could be of greater service to humanity if my process was somewhat slower. If it happened too quickly for me, I would not be able to observe it as deeply. Part of my soul's purpose, he said, was to be able to teach this, and write about this.

I was relieved, and excited about this new revelation. Somehow I had wondered if there was something wrong with me, whether I hadn't prepared enough, or wasn't worthy enough, all the countless explanations spewed up by the mind when something it thinks it wants does not happen. He assured me that there was nothing I needed to do or not do, and that it would happen soon. Somehow, in that moment, I realized that my search had already ended. My entire life had been driven by the need to help humanity move into the Golden Age, and that the next level of my work could now begin. "You have a destiny", Bhagavan told me, "and it will be fulfilled."

I believe that Bhagavan could well be a primary vehicle for the inauguration of the Golden Age. As he emphasizes, however, 'Kalki' does not refer to himself alone, but to the collective avataric consciousness that humanity is emerging into. As each of us becomes enlightened, we too enter into this Kalki consciousness. This book could be seen as the story of a particular avatar who has learned to give enlightenment to people through a neurobiological process. Yet it is also the story of an unprecedented descent of avataric presence, here to awaken all of humanity as we approach the birthing of a new Age.

Bhagavan claims that humanity is on the threshold of a mass enlightenment, perhaps similar to what Sri Aurobindo and the Mother envisioned as the descent of the 'supramental force'. He says that once a 'critical mass' of people become enlightened, then mass enlightenment will begin. Bhagavan's mission is to prepare this critical mass so they can enlighten the rest of the world. Once this happens, it will effortlessly solve the environmental, political, social and economic crisis that is looming so heavily before us today.

"Enlightenment is very easy", ended Bhagavan as we left, "and everyone should get enlightened". My hope is that this book will inspire many to do so. After all, he says, it is only the beginning of the true spiritual riches that are available to us as incarnated souls.

In the days that followed I witnessed extraordinary miracles taking place around me every day, performed not only by Bhagavan, but also by countless enlightened people, ranging from physical healings to divine assistance to rainmaking to raising the dead. The most amazing miracle of all was to watch someone going through their enlightenment process.

My research into the evolutionary history of humanity had convinced me that a Shift was imminent, and that a new species of humanity was being birthed. Here, I was seeing history unfold before my own eyes! Thousands have received enlightenment since this phase of the work began a year ago in August 2003, and the pace continues to increase exponentially.

What does this mean for each of us personally? If you have read this far, you are probably beginning to feel the echoes within your own soul calling for this divine gift. How do you begin this journey of freedom? How do you break free from the control and limitations inherent within the human condition? You may wish mull over the following statements, seeing if they resonate with you, before proceeding further:

- The human self, or ego, is programmed for separation, which is the cause of human suffering.
- Enlightenment is the shift from ego to essence.
- Enlightenment is a neuro-biological event, which can happen through grace. All the spiritual practices in the world are only a preparation for this possibility.

- The planet is in danger of extinction. Only a planetary enlightenment will save humanity.
- Grace has descended to make that possible. Enlightenment is now available for the masses.
- Thousands have become enlightened already, without years of preparation or struggle.

The world needs to know this now. There is no longer time for anything else.

3. The Process Begins

In February 2004, six months after Grace's enlightenment, we came back to Oneness University to teach at the next Experience Festival. We decided to stay on for a while afterwards so I could gather material to write this book. We observed countless numbers of people receiving the deeksha, and going through an enlightenment process. It was truly an amazing phenomenon.

Yet I still hadn't gone through my own enlightenment. When I first started writing this book, I felt I should write the bulk of it from the unenlightened state in order to relate better to where I thought people might be, and then add a chapter at the end about my own experience of it. I was also a little concerned that I might go into a non-functional state of deep samadhi for some time afterwards, and not be able to think well enough to write.

When I showed the early manuscript to one of the direct disciples of Bhagavan, and shared my reasoning with her, she pointed out that in order to truly relate to the human condition, I would need to go through my own enlightenment first. Until then I was relevant only to myself, and my own ideas of what the world needed. She noticed that I had used a lot of metaphysics, and further added that Bhagavan's teachings are not metaphysical at all; they are purely empirical. In response to my fears about not being able to write, she laughed. Without the interference of the mind's constant chatter, I would be able to focus as never before.

I recognized that underneath my questions was also an issue of trust. I had grown to rely on my mind to perform in a certain way, and was afraid that I would not have access to the same clarity and flow that I thought was 'mine'. My mind delivered a vision of losing my self and become a mindless, blithering idiot. As I shared this with her, she laughed again, and affirmed that not only would I have access to all the positive inspiration I was already familiar with, but that the entire universe could now write through me!

I realized that I was seeing the Universe as somehow separate from myself, somehow less capable of understanding and living out my destiny than I was capable of doing through my own efforts. Even though I lived much of my life from the sense of a Divine Indwelling Presence, it wasn't with total unconditional trust. I didn't fully believe that the Universe was a conscious living intelligence. A part of my mind still held on to the idea that if 'I' disappeared, then the Universe would somehow muck it up for me. I had not experienced the Universe as a divinely conscious, supremely intelligent, constantly evolving, synchronistic force of wisdom and beauty. I knew it was true, but did not experience it fully. After all my years of exploring metaphysical truths, it was still very much a concept to me.

I saw that in sharing my ideas of what was happening at Oneness University, I had relied heavily on teachings and concepts. Much as I resonated with the teachings, I had not had the direct experience, and so could only talk about them from an indirect metaphysical perspective. It was wonderful metaphysics but it wasn't direct empirical experience, and was therefore simply a concept. I realized I would have to re-write much of what I had written, and that only as I wrote from direct experience would my words have impact.

I also realized that I had a concept of God that was still subconsciously associated with punishment or indifference. I didn't quite trust that God could be my best friend and partner, and was actively interested in my highest happiness. I still believed in a God who was constantly out to 'test' me and put hurdles in my path in order to prove my worthiness and love. I still believed that I should continue to suffer 'for my highest good'. It was this version of God that prevented me from actively surrendering to my own enlightenment. It is up to each of us to design the version of God we choose to interact with, says Bhagavan, but he invites us to remember that a jealous or punishing version of God is much less likely to give us this profound gift of grace.

Within minutes of these realizations, another direct disciple of Bhagavan came to tell me that they were going to put me through the enlightenment process starting the following day. Unlike the normal 5-day courses, this would be a longer course for teachers. It would include the empowerment to transfer deeksha to other people.

There were six other people in my process group. It lasted seventeen days, and has truly been the most magical experience of my life.

I understand now that having spent my whole life studying and practicing metaphysical teachings, my mind was full of concepts about God, concepts about soul, concepts about the universe, concepts about love, concepts about what enlightenment should look like. All these got obliterated. Much of my life I had been forcing my experiences to fit into pre-existing concepts. With the concepts gone, I could now directly experience truth!

Afterwards, the book began to completely re-write itself. I decided to start with my own experiences instead of leaving them for the end. I realized that only if accompanied by personal experience would the teachings be effective. When they substitute for the experience, teachings are worse than useless; they take us even deeper into the traps of the mind. It is only while glimpsing the experience that the teachings can be truly assimilated.

I received seven 'deekshas' during the course of the enlightenment process, spread out over seventeen days. A deeksha is a hands-on transfer of power, channeled by the members/guides of Oneness University. When the deeksha is given it sets into motion a series of neuro-biological shifts within the brain. Certain areas in the frontal lobes of the brain get activated, while other areas within the parietal lobes get de-activated, eventually resulting in a totally different perception of reality known as the enlightened state. Additionally, the corpus collosum, which connects the two brain hemispheres, is energized, allowing the brain to synchronize and work together, further stimulating the 90% of the brain's functions that lie dormant in most of us.

As I received each deeksha, it very purposefully created changes in my neurobiological structure, resulting in the experience of altered states of consciousness accompanied by powerful insights. The peak experience following a deeksha usually lasts for 6-12 hours, sometimes more. During the course of one of these deekshas, I realized that what I had to do was not to write the book, but become the book. My own process and experiences during the deekshas would serve as the blueprint for anyone reading about them in such a way that the teachings could take hold, and not just the teachings, but the deeksha itself could be transferred through the sharing. But for this I would have to be transparently honest.

There is only One Mind. Even though the details of our lives are different, the content of each mind is basically the same – jealousies, longings, insecurities, passions – on and on and on. The sharing of my own process could thus also stimulate an identical process within each person, and act in some fashion as a deeksha. Perhaps this is what Bhagavan meant when he said that he wanted me to experience the enlightenment process gradually enough so I could write about it. Maybe I could teach it, even transfer it, through these writings!

This is my intention for the next few chapters. Each chapter includes some of Bhagavan's teachings, as shared by our 'guide', followed by the corresponding experience in the deeksha that followed. I have written up many of the teachings as discourses or dialogues. Although they may not be the exact words used, I felt that this would engage the reader in a more immediate way.

Later in the book I have also included a few chapters entirely devoted to the teachings of enlightenment, but hopefully by then, you will have a wider context to put those teachings into! You may even begin with those chapters if you wish, or go back and forth for deeper clarification.

I have felt Bhagavan's presence overlighting the entire process, from the timing of the process, to orchestrating my deeksha experiences, to inspiring the creative energy that flowed through these writings. Regarding my earlier fear that I would be reduced to a blithering mindless idiot after enlightenment, all I can say is that my mind has never been sharper nor more focused, never more receptive to fresh new ways of expression, never more present in each and every moment.

On your part as the reader, please enter into this journey with the intention of deeply experiencing your own responses. Perhaps you may wish to make a link with Amma and Bhagavan and invite their grace as you begin your own process. This does not need to conflict with anybody's religious beliefs. Once you experience enlightenment you realize that all these separate faces of God are part of the same Oneness, which also includes your own face. Or you may simply call upon your own conception of God or Divinity to guide your journey onwards.

There is a mantra used at Oneness University which may also prove beneficial. It is known as the 'moolamantra'. Invoking the divine consciousness of the Supreme One in all its unmanifest and manifest forms, including the avataric consciousness of Amma and Bhagavan, it goes:

"OM Satchidananda Parabrahma
Purushottama Paramatma
Shri Bhagavati Sameta
Shri Bhagavate Namaha"

~~~~~~~~~~ ✹ ~~~~~~~~~~

Friend

Ah, my friend
I see you shrouded in the mist
Reaching out your hand of light
Beckoning me to follow.
How long have you been waiting?
How long have I been afraid?
Who is the self that is afraid to die?
Soon I must run now,
Like a moth to the flame,
Like a river to the sea.
The past is real no more.
What is there to fear
When fear itself melts away
In the fires of living presence?
I look into the mist
Unveiled at last, my Friend stands before me
In blazing, undying light,
Holding out his arms,
Wearing my own face –
There is only one of us here!

~~~~~~~~~~ ✹ ~~~~~~~~~~

4. Sewers of the Mind

"The mind is like a sewer", said our teacher and guide, as he began to share Bhagavan's teachings with us. "We cover it up with a golden lid, but the stink comes through anyway. It fills the entire house, but we are so busy admiring the golden lid that we don't perceive it. We do not know who we are. The lid is composed of other people's concept of ourselves, which is the only way we know to refer to ourselves. We get attached to these images of ourselves."

"Instead of cleaning out the sewer", he continued, "we keep staring at the golden lid, which only takes us away from what we know ourselves to be, all the miserable, self-serving, loveless insecurities, comparisons, judgments, lusts, and pain that we try so desperately to cover up and mask. Someone tells us how helpful we've been, so we try and go around helping everybody, however empty we feel, just so we can feel good about ourselves. We believe we are nasty, so we project that out into the world around us, so people will treat us like we believe we deserve to be treated. We are always reinforcing our concepts about ourselves."

"These concepts are like a dead rat in the middle of the room. We sweep it under the rug, but the stink is there. So we cover it up with a bigger rug, or spray perfume into the air, but eventually the stink will come back even stronger. We need to find the rat and remove it."

"The biggest stink comes from our concepts of spirituality and enlightenment. We substitute the experience of enlightenment for concepts of enlightenment. We think enlightenment is saintliness, so we try to move towards saintliness. We think enlightenment is knowledge, so we try to move towards knowledge. We think enlightenment is perfection, so we try to move towards perfection. We lock ourselves up in the prison of our own mind – all our concepts, expectations and ideals."

"When the deeksha is given it has to break its way past all your self-concepts. If you can begin emptying out these concepts, and honestly witness the truth about yourself in your unenlightened state, that will help. Start looking at your masks and cover-ups, all your manufactured emotions, all your self-reproach, all your insecurities. It is only when you authentically see yourself for what you are that the grace can come."

"When we see ourselves in our vulnerabilities, when we allow our deepest fears to surface, we are no longer dangerous to ourselves or to others. Paradoxically, it is only when we accept our ugliness that we can be truly free. We become like a little child. We no longer need the golden lid to cover up the stink, and can go clean up the sewers instead. This is what the first couple deekshas will do," added our guide. "They will help you open up the sewers".

"Cleaning them out is simply a matter of honest observation. It is like peeling an onion. The onion is being peeled, but even when you get to the bottom, the peelings are still there. Enlightenment doesn't mean the onion disappears, it means there is no concept of an onion left to hide behind. We see our fears, but they do not rule us, we see our lusts but don't cover up, we see our insecurities, but accept them."

"We do not have to get to the bottom of our sewers," continued our guide. "That is the trauma of perfection. If we only see one of our neurotic dramas all the way through it is enough. The grace will come. Do not make another expectation about how or when it should happen."

He looked at me directly. "There is a difference between metaphysical knowledge and empirical experience," he said. "We metaphysically create the ideal of a 'soul', and create immense conflict in our minds the more we try and live up to this ideal image. The bigger our image of perfection, the further away we find ourselves, the bigger the masks we have to put on, and the more conflict and pain we suffer. The longer we are on a spiritual path the more concepts we have built up, and the harder it is to let go."

"Empirical knowledge is about being true to yourself in your experience of the moment. The more honest you are with yourself, the more you will see how the unenlightened person is built up of masks, expectations, and ideals, all of it to cover up deep insecurities and self-reproach, core loneliness, and loss of soul. Start with that, explore that. The deeper you go into this core of ugliness, the less you will feel the need to fear it, and the more you will come out of your conflict and suffering."

Our mind is such a little thing in the vastness of experience, I realized. We hold on to our little thoughts when the whole universe is rushing by. We let metaphysical concepts choke us when truth is so very simple. An enlightened person, when he looks at a tree, is simply looking at a tree. The unenlightened person builds up concepts about it, like ah, this person is in cosmic communion, he has become one with the tree! There is nothing to become. Enlightenment is to see reality as it already is.

"Sometimes we go about pitying ourselves," goes an ancient Ojibway saying, "and all the time we are being carried on great big winds across the sky."

~~~~

The first deeksha was to be given that evening. Our guide warned us again that the purpose of this deeksha was to make us examine the sewers of our mind. Until an alcoholic 'hits bottom' he cannot overcome his slavery to alcohol. Likewise, unless we fully experience the slavery of our minds, how can we seek liberation?
~~~~

As we sat in the teaching hut, two more guides came in. As they began to open up to Bhagavan's energy, they started going into high states of divine ecstasy and their bodies became channels for Bhagavan's grace. As we went forward one by one, these deeksha guides placed their hands upon our heads, and initiated the process of neurological restructuring.

After the deeksha was given we were asked to go into our rooms and lie down. Gradually, a great sense of uneasiness began to grow within me. My social persona began to dissolve, and I began to see in great detail the games I played with people in order to manipulate them and get my own way, all the while attempting to present an image of myself as kind, loving, wise, honest, and spiritual. I saw my judgments and comparisons, my jealousies and resentments, all the while desperately trying to convince myself I was spiritually evolved.

I watched my aggression and rage, then watched the suppression of my aggression and rage. I watched the conflicts within my mind as I struggled to forgive, still resentful on the outside, still plagued by guilt inside. I watched my need to be perfect, to be special, to be unique. I watched myself reacting defensively to any assault, real or imaginary, towards the cherished spiritual identity that I had so carefully built up over the years.

I began to witness with utter horror the immense insanity and 'ugliness' of my mind, which Bhagavan defines as any kind of self-centered activity. I could see this extending into even the most spiritual of motivations. Was I being good because I was conditioned to be good? Was I striving to impress someone by my saintliness? Was I helping because I was afraid to say no? Did I love because I wanted to be loved back? Did I want to be recognized for being wise or wonderful? Was I feeling so empty inside that I had to run around from workshop to workshop filling myself up with every high that came my way? Did I talk about dying to self only to use it as yet another building block in my spiritual edifice? Did I want to be in total charge of my life, even when I stated I was in service to the Divine? Did I feel the need to even achieve enlightenment by my own efforts, finally placing the crown of enlightenment upon my own head?

I saw how needy and inauthentic my entire life had been. I saw that this wonderful personality that I thought myself to be was nothing but a mind-controlled robot. As I continued to observe, I noticed that over the years I had built a whole set of identities around myself. The spiritual identity was the worst one of them all. I was a spiritual teacher and a healer. I was sensitive and compassionate. I was a good person. I had a mission to heal the world. I was wise and loving and deep. I saw that I had become so identified with this image of myself that these very identities became a mask. I found myself carefully protecting this image lest someone see through me into a place that was vulnerable or uncertain, angry or lustful, unloving or fearful, ordinary or shallow, depressed or shy.

I saw my desperate needs for approval, for acceptance, for love. I noticed how I was eating up the world around me in order to survive. More is beautiful, bigger is better. I noticed how true this was for me, whether this had to with a material identity or with spiritual experiences. I noticed how

I was dressing up my vices to become virtues. My fear of others becomes my need for 'solitude'. I cultivated 'humility' because I didn't have the courage to stand up to abuse. I 'loved' because I was too afraid to be alone. I embarked on a mission to 'save the world' because I didn't have any other planet to go to. I couldn't find any love anywhere. I recognized how unloving I really was, how fragile and hollow my ego was.

I realized that I didn't really like people. I related to them for what they could give me, whether it was love, things, money, recognition, or opportunities for advancing myself. Perhaps they recognize my light or tell me some nice things about myself. Or perhaps it gives me a chance to tell myself I'm better, wiser, more advanced, more learned, more loving than they are. Or perhaps I get to feel touched and warmed by their light, because I really didn't believe in my own.

I didn't much like myself either. I saw that I was forever comparing myself to others, and my sense of self came from how I felt others perceived me, and whether I thought I was good enough or lovable enough or beautiful enough. And so of course I had to put on my best face at all times. I had lost my sense of spontaneity and childlike wonder. I had lost my ability to live from my soul. Indeed, I doubted if I had ever really known my soul. All I knew was a spiritual labyrinth of the mind.

Then things got really insidious. Afraid of giving up its hold, the mind began to generate uglier and uglier versions of itself. I found myself experiencing enormous depression, self-condemnation, paranoia, and pain, desperately feeding this last illusion as if it were the only thing that was real. I found myself re-living the deep conditioning of 'original sin' from my teenage years. I was a worm crawling in the dust, worthy only of suffering. Indeed, it was this suffering alone that redeemed me, and the more I suffered the more I was redeemed. Suffering became the ultimate meaning of my life.

I went further back to the conditioning of my early childhood. My needs didn't matter. Others mattered only. I didn't exist for myself. I was nothing. I was powerless. I was empty. I suddenly realized that my lifelong struggle for enlightenment had its origins in this longing to give meaning to this emptiness.

That was it. I had reached the bottom of the sewage tank. There was nothing more the mind could churn up. I drifted off into sleep.

Strangely, during the course of this deeksha, I felt an enormous wave of relief each time a realization hit me. It was a relief to crawl out of my hole of self-pity and self-condemnation, it was a relief to take off the masks of spiritual ego, and it was a relief to see the ugliness of my mind so that I no longer had to maintain the struggle. I saw that the struggle was only the 'me' trying to convince itself I was good as opposed to something else that was 'not me' that I could identify as bad. I was continually projecting this 'bad' onto other people, or to outer circumstances, or to shadow aspects of myself that were somehow part of my 'subconscious self'.

When I could see myself in all my ugliness I could finally come to terms with reality. I wasn't frightened by it anymore.

I no longer needed to resist it, or even to take it personally. I even became a bit bored of the whole drama. After all, it's not even my own mind. "Strangely", our guide had said, "when you see your ugliness clearly you no longer need to act it out. When you see your ugliness clearly, you no longer need to behave ugly". When I gave up trying to 'look good', I could truly be myself. The war with the universe was over!

5. Multiple Personalities

"There are always two sides of the mind", began our guide one morning, "the good and bad, right and wrong, the ideal and the real. They are always in conflict with each other."

"We always choose the brightest of these sides and identify with it, calling this our 'self'. Everything else then becomes the contents of the self. They become 'our' thoughts; they become 'our' emotions. Enlightenment is recognizing that there is no such self, that all of these are equally our personalities."

"We are always looking at reality from a relative perspective," he continued. "A river is only defined by its banks. Our minds contain our thoughts like a pot contains pebbles. We need a relative object to define ourselves, relative thoughts to define our self. Enlightenment is breaking this container."

"We jump from one side of our mind to the other; we have hateful thoughts and then tell ourselves we shouldn't have such hateful thoughts, that we should forgive, or that they didn't mean it, or couldn't help themselves, or that they deserved it, whatever justifications or rationalizations we use to excuse our own hatefulness."

"The hatefulness is disowned, is literally not our self. We create an idealized image of ourselves, and call it our 'self'. As we study metaphysics we even call this our 'soul', and the soul becomes all good, as opposed to our thoughts and feelings, which need to be purified, and so we embark on our work of purifying our dark side, or the 'subconscious', to make it more acceptable."

I noticed my resistance to this concept. The mind doesn't like to have its illusions smashed. I didn't like to think of not having a soul, which was by definition divine and permanent. To me absence of permanence meant non-existence, and this ran counter to my most cherished beliefs about the nature of the soul and universe. Our guide pointed out that all I had was metaphysical concepts, and that I was trying to fit an experience into these concepts. It Isn't that the soul doesn't exist, he said, but before enlightenment, it is only a concept. After enlightenment, I would have an entirely new experience of it. In fact, my experience of myself would be the soul experiencing itself.

As I continued pondering on his words about the split in consciousness created by our minds, I realized that we even project this split onto our concepts of God. In most of the world's religions, God is good, wise, loving, powerful, and so on. Because we cannot conceive this God as also mirroring the negative personalities, we create the equivalent of a devil, who is conveniently and proportionately evil. As I write, I notice that 'God' is capitalized, at least in the English language, while the 'devil' is not.

Even our words for God and devil are themselves only a distortion of the words 'good' and 'evil'! What does it reveal about our collective human psyche that God is usually perceived as an authoritarian male figure? Bhagavan emphasizes that God is both male and female, depending on which aspect of God you are relating to.

"We cannot escape the negative personalities", emphasized our guide. "They are all a part of you. Our continuous effort to maintain the sense of an ideal self means that we are also continuously denying, suppressing, condemning, or projecting these negative personalities onto others and ourselves." In a flash of insight, I realized that much of my spiritual search had been about trying to escape my negative personalities. I also realized with painful clarity that many of my concepts of the soul were nothing but my mind's attempt to further elevate the self. It is the mind's way of trying to create its own enlightenment.

"We develop a seeker personality that seeks to become enlightened," continued our guide. Yet the seeker is also part of the river and doesn't know it"

"There is no person, only personalities. There is no thinker, only thoughts. After enlightenment, this is perceived very clearly. There are only bubbles of consciousness coming up, and passing away, coming up and passing away in the great silence. During the peak experience of enlightenment even these bubbles cease, and all that is left is the emptiness, the great silence, bliss. After the peak experience is over, our relationship with our mind is forever changed. There is no charge, no ownership of our thoughts, and therefore no duality. The good, the bad and the ugly all have equal residence and no residence. None of them are real anymore, none of them are fixated as the self while excluding the others as merely 'our' thoughts and emotions contained 'within' the self."

"The unenlightened person labors under the illusion that there is a continuity of self," said our guide. "There are some who believe in the reality of a self, others who believe that there is no self. Bhagavan says that self as a fixed permanent entity is an illusion; what exists is consciousness arising and falling in every moment and through every experience. When the deeksha is given, the brain is restructured in such a way that it becomes capable of observing the endless stream of personalities, each with its own mental content, each rising up, then falling away. It is like taking a 35 mm movie and slowing it down so you can begin to observe the separate frames of existence".

"When you are enlightened," he continued, "there is no more necessity to judge or compare. You witness the entire dance of creation taking place inside you, but without identifying with any of it. You recognize that each of your personalities, each seeming center of identity, is equally transient. You are not attached to the positive personalities, nor do you condemn the negative personalities. It is like bubbles of transient existence coming up moment by moment, then dissolving. Thoughts, feelings, sensations rise up, then fall away into the silence. You are no longer able to find a single continuous self that you define as 'you'."

Our guide used the example of smashing up a mirror. "Which one of these pieces is you, he asked. Or think of a spray bottle, he said. Which of these droplets of mist is you? Is there such a thing as a river separate from the water that flows through it, or a wall separate from the bricks? How then is there a self, separate from these personalities that come and go?"

I recalled the years when I worked as a psychotherapist at Pocket Ranch Institute. Many of our clients had been diagnosed with what was then called Multiple Personality Disorder. Whenever a different personality would come up, an entirely different set of personality traits would emerge. One personality could be a 3-year-old traumatized girl, another could be a teenage male protector, and another could be a 35-year-old professional artist.

Whenever a personality was up, it is as if he 'owned' the body, whenever another one came up, it was she who 'owned' the body. They were surprised and offended to realize that others were sharing the body, and especially to think that there might be a 'host personality' that may somehow include all of them.

It was like a revolving door. Each had different memories, different emotions, different perceptions of age, gender, self, and the world. Each had a different sense of their body, which even influenced their actually measurable physiology. One would have diabetes or multiple sclerosis, another would be perfectly healthy. One would have perfect vision, another be blind. One would be a public speaker, another was mute. In one instance I had heard about, even the blood type would change! The body molded itself to the individual perceptions of every personality. MPD has always been perceived as a disorder. In revealing that we are a series of personalities rather than a single fixed self, could it actually be an evolutionary advancement in response to humanity's trauma?

"Examine all the different personalities", our guide was saying. "During the course of a day, these might continually change, even moment to moment. There is no such thing as a permanent personality, just as there is no such thing as a permanent self."

I started looking at my own multiplicity. A curious and generally receptive personality shows up in class, followed by one who just wants to lie in the sun and do nothing. I feel scolded, and so a very young, shy and insecure personality comes up, and some time later a wild, aggressive one. Now the writer shows up, who can't wait to put this information down in words, accompanied by the spiritual teacher. The metaphysician shows up feeling a bit put off because his spiritual concepts have just been challenged, followed by the doubter.

Soon the seeker shows up again, driving my search for enlightenment, followed by one who is resentful for having wasted so much of his life on an empty search. Then come the commentator and the editor, taking turns to stand apart and watch the rest of the personalities revolving in and out. I want something I cannot seem to get, and the manipulator comes up, I don't get what I want, and the victim shows up. The loser, the lover, the critic, the peacemaker, the fearful, the terrorist, the martyr, the tyrant, the list goes on and on.

What is the potential for healing once we understand that all our symptoms are simply generated and contained within certain personalities? Equally, what is our potential for manifesting the divine once we become totally devoid of the sense of a separate self?

"Upon enlightenment", continued our guide, picking up my thoughts, "even the sense of body as a separate entity disappears, and is seen as simply another personality as well. When you become enlightened, you become very fluid. You are not separate from a tree, a dog, or a bird. Your boundaries dissolve. You literally become the body of the universe, for the universe to dance through!"

~~~~

That evening we received our second deeksha. As the power of the deeksha intensified, the dance of personalities became very clear. I saw that for every positive personality there was also a negative one, and that for every negative personality there was also a positive one. There were hundreds of these personalities. Some were deep-seated long-
~~~~

term personalities; others came and went only for that moment. A personality could be created from every experience in life. Now I was even creating a personality whose only job was to discover new personalities! I made a long list of these in my mind, became overwhelmed, then finally gave up.

I had come to terms with the self-centeredness of my mind during the last deeksha, so I did not feel much of a charge as I watched the negative personalities come up. The more I allowed them to be, the friendlier they seemed to become. The more I was able to perceive my mental-emotional states as distinct personalities, the less I felt attached to any one of them, and the more empty I felt of a sense of self.

I realized that when I was empty of self, the personalities could come and go fluidly. When 'I' resisted or tried to change a personality such as hurt, doubt, or anger, either by condemning it or suppressing it, the emotional charge would build up and I would start feeling uncomfortable in my solar plexus. If I noticed this emotional charge and experienced it fully, then it would soon dissipate. As the duality dissolved, which is tantamount to the dissolution of the sense of the separate self, the shadow personalities would flow back together into a unified stable configuration.

In our work with multiple personalities at Pocket Ranch, we would have the different alters begin to acknowledge each other's presence, and learn to communicate with each other. I realized that as I acknowledged myself equally as a multiple of personalities, I was loosening up the fixed 'self', and along with it the entire framework of 'ifs', 'buts' and 'shoulds' that had controlled my life.

It was an exhilarating discovery. I continued witnessing as I dropped off to sleep.

~~~~~~~~~~ ✹ ~~~~~~~~~~

Who am I?

I look out through your eyes
And see myself looking back –
Who sees who?
A lone cuckoo bird calls out to another
In the early dawn
And I hear my own voice calling back –
Coo who? Coo who?
A gentle breeze
Caresses the tall prairie grass,
A coyote howls at its sister the moon,
The night owl
Swoops towards its own shadow –
Who? Who? Who?
We are all inseparably linked,
Linked from eternity.
You look out through my eyes
And see yourself looking back –
Who sees who?

~~~~~~~~~~ ✹ ~~~~~~~~~~

6. Mind Struggle

Our guide continued the teachings by discoursing on the nature of mind. "We think we are separate minds with separate thoughts but Bhagavan says that in reality there is only One Mind. This One Mind has remained unaltered for millennia, ever since the dawn of civilization", he said. "The contents of this Mind may continually re-arrange themselves, but the structure has remained the same."

"Bhagavan says that the mind is essentially a computer that functions in certain fixed modes. There are basically four modes of this mind", he went on to say. "The 'defining' mode is continually interpreting reality through pre-existing filters. It is not happy until it has analyzed and pigeonholed reality into a form it can grasp. While looking at a tree, for instance, it is not happy until it can classify the shape, size, color and botanical name, so that it can then pretend to understand it. When looking at a concept it is not happy until it has categorized it as true, false, useful, foolish, and so on. When looking at a person it is not happy until it has determined exactly how useful or useless this person could be to oneself."

"Then there is the 'blaming' mode. Either the mind is turned outwards into blaming others, or turned inwards into blaming itself, sometimes fluctuating back and forth in schizophrenic confusion." It was not difficult to see how this worked. I blame my partner for making me late, then feel guilty for not being kind to her. I blame political figures for war on earth, then blame myself for identical patterns in my daily relationships.

The 'conflict' mode is no better. "There are always two sides of the mind functioning as opposites", he continued. Should you buy something or not? Is it better to get angry or to hold it in? It requires that you lose touch with the spontaneity of the present moment, and run every decision through the filters of your carefully constructed social persona."

"Finally", he said, "there is the 'becoming' mode. You are never happy being what you are. You cannot stay with the present moment. You are continually looking to a future psychological or spiritual goal or destiny to give meaning to your life. Seeking after enlightenment is the height of the becoming mode of mind."

"Our minds continually run back and forth between these different modes of expression", our guide commented. "It is the journey of our entire lives. We never feel and act spontaneously, and never truly love, because we are constantly separating ourselves from the reality of the moment through these filters of the mind. Not only that, our minds delight in giving us a sense of our own uniqueness, but we are really all the same. How could we not be when we are all controlled by the same Mind, the same struggles and strategies of survival?"

Our guide then read out to us the words of the ancient Indian philosopher, Shankara, describing his experience of enlightenment. To paraphrase it, he was saying, "Neither am I wind, nor water, nor earth, nor fire, nor ether. Neither am I the body, nor mind, nor senses, nor soul. Neither am I heaven nor earth nor the worlds in between. Neither am I empty nor full...." He goes on for ten stanzas, "not this, not this", and then concludes, "All these things that I am not.... That I Am!"

Essentially what he is saying is that enlightenment is not something that can be felt or understood or experienced or expressed by the mind or through words. The mind has built-in limitations that cannot be transcended. The closest the mind can get to it is paradox.

~~~~

The third deeksha was a powerful blast of energy. The silver sandals representing Bhagavan were placed on our heads followed by divine water, followed by three more guides placing their hands upon our heads. As I lay on my bed after
~~~~

the deeksha, my mind went into an intense struggle. Two hours had gone by and 'nothing' was happening.

I wondered why it was so easy for Grace and for other people, and why it was taking me so long to get enlightened. I alternated between feeling useless, angry, restless, and miserable. I felt listless, like all my energy had been drained out of the body. I wanted to just quit and go to sleep. Maybe the next deeksha will give me the zap I need, I thought with resignation.

Our guide came into the room to check in. "How are you?" he asked.

"Nothing is happening", I said.

"Are you so sure?" he enquired. He asked me to describe my state. Then he asked me what I was expecting enlightenment to look like.

As I talked I realized I was expecting enlightenment to be a high, sort of like an LSD trip, an altered state of reality where I would be struck on the head with lightning and immediately go into cosmic consciousness. I was expecting that I would experience what I imagined that Shankara had experienced, or what Buddha had experienced, or what Jesus had experienced.

Our guide made me realize that I was still carrying around a concept about enlightenment, and still expecting that enlightenment should fit into this concept. "Enlightenment is simply about seeing reality as it is," he continued, "not about choosing what reality you want to experience. Whether you are struggling or not makes no difference at all. The process will continue whether you struggle or not. These are all personalities that come and go. It has nothing to do with Bhagavan's grace. You are still trying to put enlightenment into a box."

I realized that I was still holding the expectation that I could somehow create my own enlightenment, perhaps by finding the most 'spiritual' of all my personalities, and bringing him forward. I noticed my fear that somehow I wasn't doing it right, and that therefore I would fail. I noticed I was caught up in the 'becoming' mode of the mind. How foolish I was to assume that I could in any way help or stop the process! My part was to receive the deeksha; the rest was up to Bhagavan. Understanding this made everything a lot simpler. I relaxed.

Suddenly my guide stopped me in the middle of a sentence, "Your voice quality has changed. Bhagavan's grace is here."

I started feeling an altered state coming on. He asked me to focus on my heart. "Do you feel the silence there?" As I listened, the heartbeat grew louder and louder. "The enlightenment train has left already. It will be here by 7 o'clock", he said humorously, and left the room.

As I lay in my hut, I began to experience my body dissolving. I put my fingers to my wrist in order to feel my pulse, and suddenly the pulsing expanded to fill my entire body, and then out into space. I couldn't feel the pulse in my physical body anymore. Everything was only this pulse, and I was inside it.

The next few hours I was focused entirely on this heartbeat. As I entered into it, Amma and Bhagavan were there. I felt it was their heart beating. I felt a tremendous pain in my physical heart from the intensity of their presence. It was almost more than I could handle, and I kept breathing deeply into the pain.

Every once in a while, when the energy backed off a bit, I would check to see if I could feel my physical pulse. Every time I tried to, I would once again be taken out into this huge expanded heartbeat. Sometimes the pain was so strong I thought my heart would explode, then it would back off a little, and then come back equally strong. Was this my childhood pain, I wondered? Was this humanity's pain? Was I being shown a glimpse of this so that my heart could open in compassion to the world? It didn't matter. It was all the same. All I could do was stay with the experience, which continued into the early hours of morning, when I fell asleep.

7. Letting Go

When I woke up the following morning there was a deep space within my heart. There was a silence between my thoughts, between my personalities. The silence was so deep I could drown myself in it. "Was I enlightened", I thought excitedly. I got out of bed, wobbled outside the hut to watch the sunrise, then came back in and began to journal. After summarizing my experiences of the night before, I continued to ponder:

"When there is no struggle there is a great silence, not The Great Silence, just a great silence... whenever I capitalize something it becomes a concept. i need to change the english language and remove all the capitals from it. people would be less self-important if they were simply an i. perhaps that's the cause of our entire mind disease, that we started capitalizing our self.

When you are enlightened you look at a tree, and you are the tree – simple. there is no self-important I relating to the concept of a Tree built up over a lifetime of words. no, you look at a tree, there's no you, there's no tree – so you are the tree. you don't even 'become' the tree, everything just is the way it is. An unenlightened person looks at the enlightened person looking at the tree, and comes up with all kinds of silly nonsense about Deep Communion and Cosmic Consciousness, but it's only concepts until he experiences it himself..."

There were no teachings given the following couple days. I journaled a lot, catching up on the teachings and experiences of the past few days. I was in a state of crystal clarity of mind, in which all my thoughts became extremely transparent. I could see how this state of clarity could be quite disturbing for anyone brought up with concepts of 'original sin' or a punishing God. A couple of people in my group were indeed experiencing paranoid fantasies, as all their self-judgments and assumptions of God came back to them magnified.

I could see that if my conception of God, whether consciously or subconsciously, was of a stern, judging, punishing Patriarch, it would make it extremely difficult to trust or surrender to such a God, and to the Universe as the playground of God. This concept of God is certainly a hindrance to Enlightenment. Within this concept of God, the Mind becomes a battleground for personal autonomy, where freedom is found in escaping from this punishing God.

How sad and erroneous this concept is! How much untold suffering, how many wars, have been unleashed in the name of such a God! Upon enlightenment one realizes that the Divine is simply All There Is, and each of us is a piece of All There Is. In fact, as the ancient Indian rishis understood, there is no difference between the Individual Soul, Atman, and the Universal Soul, Brahman.

Since it is the same Soul, and the same dance, there is never conflict between a personal will and a Divine will. They are two aspects of the same reality. We become a joyful expression of the Divine everywhere we go, simply because that is who we are! There is absolute trust and oneness with the Universe, which is nothing but benign, nothing but joyful, nothing but love!

Realizations such as these were moving through me as rapidly as I could write them. As the time for deeksha neared, I began to fantasize about the next deeksha. I saw myself going into cosmic consciousness and traveling through all kinds of lokas and meeting all kinds of cosmic beings and discovering all the secrets of the universe.

I fantasized instantaneously transporting myself from place to place like Babaji in the Himalayas, and giving deekshas to people, and watching miracles happening everywhere just like Christ did, and even more. I watched my spiritual personality having a heyday, while humility and equanimity threw up their hands in despair! Humor came in and told them to move over. "Let the guy have his fantasy in peace!" Which I did, until the next round...

Then it was time for the fourth deeksha. Like all the ones that were to follow, it was a strong one, with five guides laying on hands in succession!

~~~~

I lay down in my hut after the deeksha and turned off the fan. It was so noisy, and I had been experiencing such a deep silence, that I wanted to hang on to it, despite the summer heat. That was my first mistake, wanting to hang on to a state. I then started breathing into my heart in order to reconnect with the experience of the One Heart from my previous deeksha. That was my second mistake. Why expect to have the same experience twice?

For the longest time, nothing happened. As usual, all my personalities of doubt, frustration, self-criticism, self-pity gathered around. In fact, they came back even stronger because I had been feeling so good and enlightened before the deeksha. Then came guilt. Maybe I had just setting myself up for a fall with all my spiritual fantasizing. Or maybe it was all my training in 'original sin'. My mind began to chatter fluently. I decided to turn the fan back on to drown out the chatter in my head.

Our guide came in. "Were you expecting the big experience?" he asked me right away. I nodded sheepishly. I admitted my fear that I wasn't enlightened, and would never get enlightened. I also admitted my expectation that somehow today's experience needed to be more intense, bigger, and deeper, to prove that I was enlightened.

"How do you know that's what you need?" asked our guide. "Your mind has this concept about enlightenment",
~~~~

he went on. "You are still wanting to arrange your experiences to fit your concepts about enlightenment".

He reminded me that Bhagavan is not interested in the contents of my mind, whatever they are, only that I experience it fully. "It is better that you authentically experience frustration or self-doubt than to have the best high possible and get attached to it!"

I noticed that because of all my expectations and inner conflicts I was not able to experience what was truly here in this moment. "You are not always where you seem to be", he went on. "It's like a circle. Sometimes the shortest path is the long way around, as long as you keep walking. The mind's struggle with struggle creates an attachment that keeps you stuck there."

He reminded me that the mind was not going to change upon enlightenment, as most people believe. No, Bhagavan says that the mind will always be the mind, as ugly or self-centered as ever before, but enlightenment means being able to de-clutch from it. "Are you still weighted down with concepts about what this meant? Look at what you have been doing – identifying your personalities, dissolving the concept of self – could you do this so easily before?"

I argued with him. "Yes, I could do this before. I couldn't always change how I felt, but I could always step back and notice my stuff, even if I wasn't calling them personalities. Are you telling me this is all that enlightenment is about? If that were it, I was already enlightened even before I came here".

As I continued to argue with him, the energy started shifting. I wasn't struggling with struggle anymore. I was caught up in a huge torrent of energy, and dissolved into it.

Later my guide came back in. "Enlightenment is the most karmically loaded word there is". As I looked at him uncomprehendingly, he continued "All the struggles people have had to seek enlightenment or to get enlightened have become tied up with it. It's like going to the enlightenment website, www.enlightenment, and finding www.struggle instead. All the struggle you are experiencing is part of the field around it."

This was an interesting revelation! "There are so many teachings today, so many different kinds of sadhanas and practices, so many paths to get there, but without enlightenment these only manage to generate more craving – craving for enlightenment. The early rishis considered it a sin to talk about enlightenment if they couldn't deliver it. This is why there is such a dense karmic field of frustration and struggle surrounding it."

"Did you have the same struggle with it?" I asked. "No, Amma showed me this, and then it happened easily!"

"Why is it so easy for some people?"

"Only the very brave or the very foolish think they can take on this struggle and change it", he commented wisely. "The rest just receive it as a gift".

It was at this point that I realized that this was the form my book would have to take, these conversations with my guide. "People need to relate directly to the experience, not just get a bunch of teachings" "Yes, Bhagavan is writing the book", he affirmed. "You are the book".

After he left the heartbeat came back, and with it the pain. It was just as intense as before. I continued breathing into it, allowing myself to feel it fully. For hours, there was nothing but this heartbeat, and the pain. Gradually, towards the early hours of dawn, it subsided, and I drifted into sleep.

8. Crossing the Finish Line

The next day I asked my guide about the pain in my heart. "Don't get excited by the idea that it's the weight of the world." He related an experience where he had once told his inner Bhagavan that all he wanted to do was to help him ease the burden that he was carrying for humanity. Bhagavan said no, please, don't ask for that, but it was too late, he was already feeling the anguish.

After the pain subsided, Bhagavan told him that the best way he could help was to be joyous, and to help others get enlightened. "People get stuck with an idea of compassion," he said. "If someone was drowning in quicksand, would you want to go and join him in your so-called compassion?

Wouldn't you want to find a rope and quickly pull him out? Experiencing true compassion from an enlightened state is very different from conceptualizing about it."

Did I have some kind of an Atlas syndrome, where I wanted to take on the weight of the world in the hopes of transmuting it? Or some kind of martyr complex where I was willing to sacrifice myself for the world? No matter, it wasn't important. It was given to me for a reason, and I accepted that.

We usually had some days off between successive teachings and deekshas. Even though I was receiving powerful insights and experiences during this time, I could not maintain the states, and my mind would return to its habituated patterns of struggle, questioning, and doubt.

I didn't question the fact that I had had enlightenment experiences, but I was still struggling with the question of whether I was permanently enlightened yet. All that I remember experiencing in my last two deekshas was pain, and even that was now becoming a distant memory. There had been no bliss or cosmic consciousness, no involuntary movements of the body, no hysterical laughter as I suddenly saw the great cosmic joke, no journeys to other 'lokas' (heavenly realms), no extraordinary phenomena. I still hadn't seen any visions. "If you're asking the question, you're not enlightened", our guide had said once, so I mustn't be enlightened, but then didn't he also say that the enlightenment train had arrived?

As I talked with him I began to see the subtle games my mind was playing. I had been on a spiritual path all my life, doing intense sadhana for 20 years. How could I let go now and risk that I would suddenly get enlightened outside of my own efforts? I still needed to feel in control, even to defining and analyzing my experience of enlightenment!

"It is difficult for spiritual people to let go into enlightenment," said my guide paradoxically. "The mind wants to take credit for itself, make all that spiritual work count. What would all the years of meditation be worth if suddenly enlightenment could just be handed over to you? Enlightenment is a warrior's path. You work for it as you need to, but when it is all over and done you can't take credit for it. 'You' are dead."

He related the story of Bhagavan's driver, who was given the deeksha and immediately got enlightened. His guide asked him what the experience was like. Not having any sophisticated concepts to describe it, all he could say was, "Before, I was driving the car. Now, the car is driving itself."

I recognized that I was still struggling to hold on to the wheel, trying to understand every step of the journey. Bhagavan was telling me to shift over and let him drive, relax and enjoy the ride, or just have an ice cream cone or something, and I was saying no, I need to see where I am going, I need to control the journey, I need to drive myself into enlightenment.

All I was doing was driving myself up a wall.

~~~~

The fifth deeksha was given. Again, nothing seemed to be happening for a while. This time I knew the territory,
~~~~

however. I realized that even this perception of nothing was a mental concept. I relaxed into fully experiencing each changing personality, and soon felt myself going into an altered state. I began experiencing a deep silence.

I had been working with a practice called the 'sound current' for many years, and was familiar with a quality of silence that was quite profound. But I had never felt anything quite like this. The sound of this silence filled the entire universe!

My guide came in. "The wave and the ocean are not two," he commented. "Thoughts and silence are not separate. Silence lives below every thought, and pervades everything. It does not matter whether you are speaking or listening, walking down a busy street or meditating."

"It's like one wave watching another wave," I responded. "But it's the same ocean underneath".

"Yes, and self is an illusion that thinks it is separate from the ocean."

I had always thought of the act of 'witnessing' as somehow stepping outside myself, and watching the rest of me go by. I asked him about this.

"No, that is just another personality", he said. "Witnessing is not a separate thing. It means to not resist the changing nature of the mind, to consciously be with whatever is happening".

"In other words, you're talking about 'beingness' like the tide that continually comes in and goes back out". I told him I didn't like the term 'witness' in this context, that I preferred to just call it beingness.

"Yes", he affirmed. "But you can't even really make a distinction between beingness and oneness. When you are being, you are one. When there is no 'self' and no 'other', you are one. It is not a metaphysical oneness where you somehow 'enter into' or 'become' something or someone, but a recognition that it is the same ocean, the same silence that hangs between you."

I became distracted. Was I the drop or the ocean, was the age-old question. Was I the drop merging into the ocean or the ocean merging into the drop? I realized that even this was a meaningless analogy; even the drop is an illusion! "Which of these droplets is you", I recalled the words of our guide.

My mind returned to his words. "When you are totally being with the nature of the mind, seeing how everything just bubbles up and dies away, no sequence, no order, just random thoughts and emotions that come and go, this very being is witnessing. You don't have to forcefully pop out of yourself to see it. You are simply with it, like a cork bobbing in the waves. The concept of self is what tries to keep the cork from bobbing, keep it fixed."

Then his voice became more forceful, "You are at the finish line, Kiara".

"But it's so normal", I protested.

"Of course. It's still the same mind. You're not changing the mind; you're just not resisting it. Actually, it doesn't even matter if you are resisting or not resisting. Even that can be seen as the flow of the mind. When you're witnessing, you're not fixated in one part of the duality."

"Being means that there is no conflict", he continued. "You free up your energy. This energy is bliss."

I could see now what he had meant earlier when he said that any emotion, fully experienced, is bliss. When we can fully accept any of our personalities, conflict ceases. When conflict ceases, all the energy that was locked up in the struggle gets released, and shoots up the kundalini channels, causing bliss!

"When you're in doubt, experience the doubt", our guide advised. "When you're in resistance, experience the resistance. Beingness means you simply experience the mind directly rather than interpreting it through fixed concepts".

I realized that it was not reality itself, but our interpretations of reality that were so oppressive. It is not our suffering but our attempts to escape from suffering that cause us so much pain.

"It is like you're late for an appointment," our guide continued. "The reality is that you're late for the appointment. But then your mind jumps in to interpret it – you're stupid, you can't be trusted, you never show up on time – and pretty soon you're not just late but miserable as well. Plus, all the times in your life that you've been late, and all the times in your life that you ever felt the way you feel now, start piling up. It's a wonder more people don't go out and shoot themselves!"

"The concept of a self is the dividing line between inner and outer reality", he spoke again after a lengthy silence."

Intrigued, I asked him what he meant. "There is really no inner or outer," he pronounced. "That is why a mystical vision can be as real as or more real than physical reality. When you lose your self you become part of the playground of God, whose expression is both physical and mystical."

"Many people consider that the physical world is an illusion. This may be true from a metaphysical perspective, but from an empirical perspective it is utter nonsense. This is where the debate between science and religion often gets bogged down. 'How can you say this table is an illusion,' says the empirical voice of science, 'when all my senses indicate that it is right here in front of me?'"

"Rather, it is our perception of the world that is an illusion. It is an illusion because the perceiver is an illusion. The sense of self derives its existence from the configuration of our human neuro-circuitry. When the deeksha is given, it alters this neuro-circuitry and dissolves this illusory sense of self. This is why Bhagavan says that enlightenment is a biological process."

"When the self disappears, we see reality as it is. When the self disappears, the dividing line between physical reality and mystical reality also disappears. We recognize that it is not the physical world that is an illusion but the perception that the physical world is separate from the mystical worlds which is an illusion."

"When people become slaves to the idea that the mystical worlds are more profound than the physical worlds, they naturally distance themselves from truly experiencing the physical reality around them. Even enlightenment is made into a highly mystical experience when all it means is to be in touch with what is really there."

I realized this was where I had become stuck. I had equated enlightenment with perpetually living in mystical reality, an assumption which arose from my perception that physical reality was somehow inferior to mystical reality. This perception, in turn, removed me from the reality of the present moment, in which mystical and physical realities were one.

"When there is no self, your mind simply becomes another sense", our guide continued. "Watching a thought is like watching a tree. Watching a tree is like watching a vision. They are all equally real, and they are all equally unreal."

This was a profound revelation to me. I could see that if people could really grasp this we would be living in a heaven on earth. It would mean completely disconnecting from the consensus reality of the Ancient Mind, and our relationship with matter itself would be very different. It would mean that all the insights of quantum physics would become true, not just on a micro level, but in the macrocosm as well!

While I was pondering the implications of this statement, I suddenly heard him say, "Where is the rule that says every question must have an answer? 'Am I enlightened', you ask. When you realize that doubt itself is nothing to be feared, then that question does not need to be answered."

"You have been dancing around the finish line ever since your third deeksha", he declared authoritatively.

I suddenly realized that I had been expecting enlightenment to be sort of like a huge LSD experience that would get me out of the mind. It wasn't about getting out of the mind, but paradoxically, about fully accepting the nature of the mind. Once I see it I am no longer bound by it. Once I can see the mind clearly, it loses its power to fix me in duality. Then Supreme Intelligence can come through moment by moment.

I saw very clearly that with all my concepts and expectations about enlightenment I was resisting the acknowledgement that something very powerful had taken place inside my consciousness. It was a subtle shift, but the implications were huge. I had generally been feeling at peace with myself in my life, so the contrast was less than for someone in obvious pain, but I could feel an indescribable quality of peace, silence, and attunement with life that wasn't there before. It was a peace that arose from the ability to embrace the here and now as a gift from the universe.

I saw very clearly that enlightenment does not have to be a mystical experience of being bowled over by cosmic consciousness. It is simply the realization that the concept of self is illusory, a fixation in the sea of constantly changing personalities. I also saw very clearly that in losing this fixation, I had made room for the whole universe to dance through me. What felt like a death to the mind was in actuality the ability to truly live for the first time, to truly experience reality without the constant interruptions and interpretations of the mind.

As with many people who have been on a spiritual path, I was already familiar with much of this territory. I was in touch with my soul already, and had already experienced a great deal of love, peace, and joy in my life. I already felt a sense of deep purpose. But I still felt trapped and submerged in the field of duality, however subtle the form of it. I was still feeling separate from the world, and therefore powerless in my need to change it, or change myself, to fit into my ideal of how it should or shouldn't be.

Something had changed now. I could acknowledge the perfection of all life now, even in all the seeming imperfections inherent in the world around me and within me. A great gratitude for Amma and Bhagavan welled up in my heart. I had crossed the finish line.

~~~~~~~~~~ ✸ ~~~~~~~~~~

The Garden

I see a garden beyond the flame
To enter I must burn away
Everything I have ever identified with,
All the stories I have ever told,
Everyone I have ever known or loved,
All ideas of separation and loss,
Even my yearnings for union.
I must enter empty-handed,
Expecting nothing,
Offering everything I am in return,
Offering my death to the flames.
Such a small price to pay,
So easy now
To enter the gardens of life.

~~~~~~~~~~ ✸ ~~~~~~~~~~

9. Darshan with Amma

The following day we were invited as a group for a darshan with Bhagavan. As we sat in meditation, my body dissolved into joy, and I felt giddy as a drunken pigeon for hours afterwards. It was all the proof I needed, if I needed more, that something powerful had shifted inside me.

The following day, we traveled to Nemam, where Amma does her darshans. Although I haven't spoken of Amma very much yet, Amma and Bhagavan are a single avataric consciousness in two bodies. I had asked our guide once why I didn't feel the same connection with Amma as I did with Bhagavan. He said that I probably needed to resolve something in relationship with my own mother. I knew it was time to change that.

We first attended a public darshan with Amma. There were thousands of people gathered, and their deep devotion and connection with Amma was quite touching to witness. I began to feel the vastness of her being, and went into a state of expanded joy.

Then we were called for a private darshan with her. There must have been about fifteen of us in the room, and several guides. When Amma came into the room, I felt a wave of love moving into me. Amma spoke with each one of us and gave us her blessing.

If Bhagavan's mission is about imparting the state of enlightenment, Amma out of her compassion for people, has chosen to fulfill the desires of their hearts before they seek enlightenment. Unless desires are fulfilled, most people will not have an intense seeking for enlightenment. Ordinary human desires are not to be belittled. The divine grace of Amma and Bhagavan comes to the aid of people seeking mundane desires as much as for those seeking enlightenment. We were invited to make any requests of Amma we desired.

When my turn came I dedicated my life to her work of healing and blessing the Earth. I asked that her presence be strong within me, and that Grace and I be used powerfully as vehicles for Amma and Bhagavan's grace as we traveled, taught, and gave deeksha wherever we were invited to. I could see that sharing this blessing was going to become my life. I asked that she use my hands and my feet to bless the world. I also told her about this book I was planning to write, and asked for her blessing that the book itself would become a deeksha to liberate many.

She smiled, and I felt the enormous vastness of her being. I felt how an avatar's consciousness pervades the entire cosmos, and that I was a cell within her body, one player within her dream. I understood that the miracles of healing and grace, which were reported to be happening on a daily basis in her presence, were simply an expression of her immensely giving nature. "I will do it", she said to me, as she placed her hands on my head to bless me.

I was thrown into a very deep silence that enveloped my physical body. It was hours before my body could move.

After meeting Amma I had been regretting that I hadn't asked her for certain things – such as opening my heart more fully, the gift of healing, the opening of mystical vision, and blessings for my family. Our guide told us that Amma reads all your wishes and thoughts, spoken and unspoken. Her very nature is to give, give, give...

He also told us that divine grace will start manifesting through our bodies as gifts of healing and mukti, whatever was needed in order to most effectively help people. "It is Amma and Bhagavan themselves who are now anchored in your Antaryamin (Indwelling Divinity), and will bring through these gifts."

10. Cosmic Consciousness

The following day we had our sixth deeksha. As I went into the deeksha it was with immense gratitude to Amma. I was so grateful to have met her in Nemam, to balance out the relationship I already had with Bhagavan. I kept repeating, Amma, Amma, Amma...

A few minutes into the process, lying in my hut, I heard a taxi pull up, and Grace's voice floated in. She had been gone for the past several days so I could do my enlightenment process without being distracted, and had returned earlier than I expected. I was just beginning to go into an altered state, and I felt irritated and interrupted. I stumbled out in my deeksha daze and lay on the steps of the hut next door. It was locked but I knew it was empty.

Soon, a reorganization took place in my consciousness. I realized there were no accidents, no interruptions, no separation. All things were in Amma's hands. When my guide came with the keys to the hut to let me in, I was already feeling a deep gratitude for the cosmic order of things. I relayed to him my process. "There is no separation. Everything is sacred and perfect," he affirmed.

I asked Amma to come into my heart, continuing to surrender, continuing to invite her in deeper. Soon I dissolved into an expanded state. I was no longer Kiara asking Amma to come into his heart, but Amma, inviting Kiara into hers! If she were to come into mine, I could push her out, but where else could I go if once I was held within her embrace?

The state continued to deepen. I felt bigger and bigger as my sense of body extended further and further out. I didn't have to try and feel love anymore, I was love.

I found myself giving deeksha to people I knew. My right hand lay on the bed and strong currents would start streaming out as I visualized people. I would feel their suffering in my/her body, then after a while I would feel something transform in them, and eventually the current would trickle to a halt. As I continued giving deeksha to more and more people, it happened quicker and quicker, until eventually with just a thought the current would pulse through and go where it was needed to go.

I then found myself giving deeksha to several people at once. I blessed the world leaders, even those I thought were a menace to the world, and felt the currents flow. They too are part of divine order, I realized with joy. There was no one outside Amma's grace.

Soon I was blessing entire countries, the mass consciousness of humanity, and Earth herself. When my guide next came I was in a state of cosmic ecstasy. Everything was my body; worlds and universes were being birthed in me, dissolving in me. As I breathed out, there was creation. As I breathed in, there was dissolution. I felt vast, vast, vast.

After a while, my guide came in. "Jagat Mata," I mumbled to him. "You're feeling Jagat Mata?" he asked. "No, I am Jagat Mata, Universal Mother".

After some time, my thoughts turned to Bhagavan. I felt him walking down to the lawn for his evening darshan. I likewise went through the stages of seeing him coming into my heart, then entering into his heart, and then dissolving into his cosmic presence. Soon I was Jagat Pita, Universal Father.

I first experienced Bhagavan as the Sun, literally as the physical embodiment of solar consciousness, then expanding further out yet into the endless galaxies. Again, worlds creating worlds, dissolving worlds. I experienced Amma and Bhagavan both containing and expanding each other.

I had been feeling somewhat split about my loyalties between them. Now I could see that Amma was inside

Bhagavan, who was inside Amma, like the image of the yin-yang symbol, or like a continuously turning 'tube torus'. They were not separate.

I felt the immense power of Bhagavan. When I was describing it to my guide later, my voice came from deep inside me somewhere as I smashed my fist into my open palm. I could feel the immense energy contained within the body of Bhagavan, waiting to release itself to liberate humanity.

I saw that he could dispel all darkness on Earth in one instant. But it is happening gradually in accordance with cosmic law; gradually enough so that everyone will make it. I knew in that moment that nothing could hold back his 'sankalpa', his divine intention, for world enlightenment. I had wondered how he could know with such absolute conviction – amidst all the uncertainties of the day, amidst all the environmental, political, and human crises that grow more and more depressing by the hour – that we wouldn't destroy ourselves as a human species.

I could see now that the entire world is his dream, his dance, and that the entire stream of history was a response to a divine evolutionary impulse. And I knew with an absolute certainty that our journey into the Golden Age was assured, and would happen as his grace intended.

Just like I had with Amma, I found myself giving mukti deeksha to people. Unlike Amma's deeksha of grace, however, this was a more selective process. As a few people came to mind, currents of energy would stream out of my hands. When my mind would come up with others, no energy flowed. Two or three people got the full dose, and I will be curious to find out what they experienced. The deeksha had its own divine intelligence.

I realized there was no Kiara left anywhere. Bhagavan and Amma were everywhere and everything. My body was going into spontaneous movement all by itself. I stood and danced the dance of Shiva. At times the energy would be so intense I would have to back off from it, take a few deep breaths, and then re-engage.

Often in the past, when I led group meditations, we would go through a process of expansion in our subtle bodies - merging with the group soul, then the soul of the local bioregion, then the national soul, then the planetary soul, then the galactic soul... further and further out. It would lead to a point where I felt like the stars would become the cells in my cosmic body. But that was an experience which I had only felt in my subtle bodies. I had never felt this in my physical body, never felt that I could open my eyes and dance, and the universe would dance with me! It was ecstatic beyond words!

"You had asked for cosmic consciousness", said my guide next time he checked in. "Is this intense enough for you?" I realized it was about as much as my body could handle.

"That's still not 1 percent of what they hold in their bodies all the time", he said. "As avatars, their bodies are wired differently."

An avatar's function is to bring new evolutionary potential into the mass consciousness of a species. Is this how our bodies will be wired in future generations? Is this what the ones being called the indigo children or the crystal children are preparing for?

I felt how all the avatars who had ever walked on Earth came from this same center of avataric consciousness. There was no separation between any of them. It was all a single consciousness, and each one of us is now being called into this consciousness. What I was experiencing was the same consciousness that Bhagavan embodied, not equal to his, but the same. I could now understand what Bhagavan meant about the unity of all things. We are each the same vast avataric presence here on Earth to heal and enlighten the planet. As each person becomes enlightened, they each become part of this avataric consciousness, whether we call it Kalki consciousness or Christ consciousness or Buddha consciousness!

I knew also Amma and Bhagavan's grace as it is manifesting today is not even a tiny fraction of what they are capable of giving humanity, and will give humanity in the years to come. Even this tiny fraction is bringing about a huge phenomenon of change. "How much are they capable of holding", I mumbled stupidly.

"It all depends on what's needed. As much as they need to."

I know that as we move towards global enlightenment, that this will continue to increase. The more people that become enlightened, the stronger will become the 'morphogenetic fields' of enlightenment, through which they can bring even more through – until mass enlightenment takes place!

I see this could well be a planetary ascension, not just enlightenment. But that's still ahead – we shall see. I also know that what Bhagavan and Amma are here to accomplish is much bigger than the Earth. I don't have words or concepts to imagine what this may be, but it feels cosmic in nature.

I found that as I turned my body counter-clockwise, the energies would heighten significantly, like the physical body was becoming an antenna for more of the cosmic energies to anchor down into Earth. At one point, as I danced under the stars, I could see that the stars were all part of my body's dance. They weren't stars like I normally see them. They were cells in my body, as I am a cell in Bhagavan's body. I was reminded of the beautiful metaphor of Indra's net, where the entire universe is made up of pearls, and each pearl is reflected within every other pearl, and is every other pearl. It was something like that.

"This is only the beginning," said my guide. "Your state will continue to deepen even beyond this. It will happen naturally. There is no Kiara now to make it happen or to hold it back now. It is only Amma and Bhagavan working through you".

I began to understand about divine personalities, not just them but others as well. They could come now and anchor into the Earth's frequency fields through this hollow reed that is Kiara's body. I have long felt a connection with Sanat Kumar, one of the cosmic beings who serves as a guardian for the Earth. I invited him to come through, and felt a vast consciousness take hold. It was different from Bhagavan's; I can't quite interpret it all yet, but it stayed for a long time, and I felt the Earth embraced within his body.

Then Babaji came through. I had developed a strong relationship with him over the years, ever since 1985 when I first experienced him through an enlightenment experience. For months afterwards, I had felt his energies coursing through my body almost 24 hours a day. Now I felt him again. He slid right into the physical body, and it seemed to fit him perfectly, as if it was made for him. Perhaps it is, I don't know. I only know that I am a dancing river of joy, not separate from the universe.

Finally, at one point, as I tried to engage my mind to think about how to put a sheet on the musty bed of my new hut, there was a violent reaction in my solar plexus – and I ended up puking over the porch wall. I felt an abrupt shift. It was like I had gone down through a thin curtain. No longer was I unified with cosmic consciousness. I was still held within the vast embrace of Amma and Bhagavan, but I wasn't one with them anymore.

I could understand now what Jesus meant when he said, "I and the Father are one". It is the experience of cosmic consciousness. When he says, "I am the way, the truth and the life", it is not the personal Jesus that is speaking; it is the cosmic consciousness speaking through his body.

The following morning, thoughts were back, but not in the old way. Kiara was back, but not in the old way. I wrote in my journal, "Before I was one. Now I am not-one. But I am not two either. I can understand Shankara's experience now. My hand moves as my mind moves me. Consciousness itself moves me, not some fixated little self that was illusory to begin with. My body is an empty shell for the whole universe to use. Meanwhile, the biological consciousness permeates it and empowers it. The body is such a sacred thing. It is a temple for the Holy Spirit. I understand this for the first time now. I must take care of it.

Empty yes, but oh so full – not stuffed with the measly concerns of a petty non-existent self anymore – but as full as the entire universe!

There is no person now. Kiara is empty."

11. Empowerment

The day after this experience of cosmic consciousness was a strange one for me. After experiencing the perfection and order of the cosmos, it was difficult to come to terms with the imperfection and mundane quality of human life. Why was everybody talking about such inconsequential stuff? Why did people have to whine about everything all the time?

I realized that there is always balance in the universe. After the experience of expansion, my consciousness was now going into a contraction, and all the old pathways of judgment and comparison held in my body were being stimulated. Once I could see it for what it was, the feeling gradually dissipated. I realized that there is an order and perfection even in all the seeming contradictions and imperfections.

I spoke with our guide about it. "There is perfection in the world of duality too, but only after you accept the ugliness of the mind, and no longer have a need to be living out an ideal. That is why Bhagavan says these two foundation stones are so important – ugliness of mind, and the impossibility of changing the mind. If this foundation is strong, you can go as high as you please, and you won't come crashing down. Once you get it, you no longer need to suffer emotional downswings, because depression only comes when you expect that you can change the mind and make it better. We simply see reality as it is, and are not attached to any one version of ourselves which we have to have to feed, protect or defend."

"An enlightened person doesn't have to be a saint. The Buddha lost his temper on several occasions. Nor are all saints enlightened, for that matter. It's two totally separate things."

He went on to talk about the difference between enlightenment and God-realization. God-realization means simply to have a direct experiential connection with God "An enlightened person is not always God-realized. Nor is a God-realized person necessarily enlightened. The Buddha was enlightened but he wasn't God-realized. All craving stopped when he discovered the absence of self, even the craving for God. He experienced the emptiness of self, but did not go on to experience the fullness of God. Many Sufis and poet-saints of India, on the other hand, were God-realized but they were not enlightened. They were so intent on loving God that they couldn't wish for anything more."

"Wouldn't union with God be an equally, if not more profound realization?" I asked.

"Perhaps, but they weren't interested in that. They feared that enlightenment would dissolve the self, which would put an end to their dualistic attitude of service and devotion to the Divine. The Vaishnavite saints known as 'alvars' were so intoxicated in the bliss of God-realization that they even sung in their songs, "I don't want mukti!" They preferred that God be other than themselves."

"Enlightenment without God-realization," he said surprisingly", may manifest love and wisdom but it does not manifest power. In the past God-realized beings have been able to manifest miracles, while merely enlightened beings have only succeeded in altering erroneous perceptions or giving the teachings of liberation, not actually liberating people. Miracles have only occasionally happened around them."

In the past, people have become either Enlightened or God-realized, but very rarely both. Bhagavan is doing something that has not been done before. What he is bringing is the marriage between Enlightenment and God-realization, the unity between wisdom and devotion. It is this unity that manifests as power, the power to heal, and to transfer states of enlightenment that is being widely experienced with the deeksha. Collectively, it is the power to create new worlds. We become the doorway to eternity, the fulcrum for the transmutation of the universe!

A couple days later, we went through an empowerment ceremony, where we were given a deeksha empowering us to give deeksha to others. Every time we place our hands on people's heads with intent, Amma and Bhagavan's energies would flow through us to heal, give peace of mind, or transfer enlightenment, depending on what is requested. I felt an immense gratitude as the ceremony progressed. It was the fulfillment of a longing to help humanity which I had experienced ever since I was a child. When I read the gospels of Christ as a teenager I had been profoundly impacted by the Book of Acts, where the disciples of Jesus are "baptized by the Holy Spirit" to teach, heal, and perform miracles in the name of Christ.

I felt now the same excitement in my soul as I imagine those disciples must have felt. Even more, perhaps, for this was the first time in human history that an avatar had incarnated who could actually transfer states of enlightenment to people, not just some people, but to anyone who asked, with no strings attached! It was with gratitude and awe that I realized that we were being asked to serve as extensions of his avataric presence in the world! We were individually blessed and given a 'mala' as a symbol of Bhagavan's empowerment.

Immediately after the empowerment ceremony, we were given a deeksha. It was quite gentle, and I didn't have any major insights or experiences. We were told it was a stabilization deeksha designed to better integrate our state of enlightenment. The state has continued to deepen since then.

12. Life after Enlightenment

I had always seen enlightenment as the end of my spiritual journey, the ultimate in human attainment. Now I see that it is merely a new beginning. Consciousness has its own intelligence, its own cycles, and it is an endless journey of discovery.

What happens after the peak experiences stabilize? What does 'normal' reality look like afterwards? How is this different from my normal reality before enlightenment?

It is very difficult to gauge this change. I don't have much of a reference point anymore for my life prior to enlightenment. I think of what it was like to engage in human drama, and I just can't seem to be able to go there. It is like waking up from a dream, and realizing that while the dream reality has some similarities to waking reality, it is also very different.

At the same time, many things are the same. Just because I am not identified with a fixed self does not mean I am some blob of consciousness floating around without an identity. I am still Kiara, the same memories, the same blend of personalities, except that Kiara is no longer caught up in a treadmill of mental chatter and noise. I was already pretty much at peace with myself; already felt a lot of fulfillment in my work and relationships, already felt that I was contributing a lot to the world, so these things have not changed.

What has changed are my motivations. I am no longer struggling to be at peace, struggling to make relationships work, struggling to change the world. It is rather an effortless way of life, based on the recognition that I am not in charge anymore, that there is a divine perfection at play that is far bigger than my capacity to understand or control it, and that I am simply a hollow reed in service to this divine play.

The most notable change is the deep silence I feel throughout the day. The silence does not depend on external factors. It does not matter whether I am talking or writing or thinking or meditating. This silence is here to stay. It is the undercurrent of everything I now experience.

I have had a practice of meditating with the 'sound current', a tone experienced inside the head, which takes you into deeper states of consciousness. I had never been able to get beyond a certain depth, however. Now, in this deep silence, the sound current takes me into vast realms of joy.

I experience this silence as the absence of 'static' in the mind. It is like exchanging a pair of crackling speakers with a studio quality sound system. When I pay attention to this silence, it opens up the door to an endless creative flow. I started writing this book soon after my enlightened process ended. The creative energy came through strongly, and I followed it, writing for hours at a time without tiring and without pausing. Within a week, most of it was written. The silence was the source of this inspiration, and I felt an immense joy in expressing from it. I could understand now what Simon and Garfinkel meant by 'the sounds of silence'!

Our guide was forever reminding me that enlightenment is nothing but de-clutching from the mind. The silence is the sound of this de-clutchment!

Instead of a single, continuous stream of identity, I now experience myself as bubbles of consciousness rising and falling with the silence underneath. An emotion or a thought comes up, remains for a while, and then disappears into the silence. Another emotion or thought comes up, remains for a while, and again disappears into silence. When the mind is needed, it is extremely focused and efficient. When it isn't needed, I return into the silence.

These bubbles of consciousness could be anything. It surely does not mean I am free from frustration or anger or irritation or hurt. I realize that I had a misconception that enlightenment means instant saintliness. No, all these emotions still come and go as before. The difference is that where previously that would become my identity, now I simply watch them come up, and watch them disappear. I no longer feel the need to judge them or judge myself. I am no longer identified with saintliness.

I notice that life continues around me. Things happen that are distressing, situations that I'd rather avoid. My senses are more acute, so I am more susceptible to noise and pollution, but strangely, I notice that while I still have preferences, I don't have the same reactive emotional 'charge' around these things. Whether it is noisy streets or complaining neighbors, family squabbles or world events at large, I notice a deeper sense of equanimity. There is an ability to 'switch off' from the emotional reactivity. Sometimes I get upset about things, but it is like watching someone else going through an old habit pattern of mind. As soon as I become aware of it, it begins to change. I notice that I have more choices, and am not controlled by moods and emotional swings. The ability to de-clutch from human drama seems to deepen over time, although it is not always instant or easy.

Another misconception about enlightenment I had carried is that there would be an instant flowering of psychic gifts and inner vision, or that I would forever dwell in cosmic consciousness. This has not been so. I notice, however, that my craving for these things has disappeared in the recognition that all things come in their right season. With the narrow identity of a fixed self gone, I see that I am a channel for the entire universe to flow through, and that these gifts and states will come and go as needed. There is no sense of lack here, no sense that I have to hold on to something, even the highest states of samadhi.

There is no more trying to meditate. Or to say it differently, all my life is now a meditation. Much of my need to meditate earlier was to stop the clutter in my mind so that I could attune to a deeper vastness. This is my normal state now, and I am able now to experience as deep a state of consciousness in two minutes of stillness than after an hour of meditation before enlightenment. My need to meditate had come from the striving to become something more. Yes, there is a lot further to go, especially as I observe some of the ecstatic states that the guides go into on a regular basis, but I am no longer craving these states like I did before. This moment is profound enough! Every moment is.

I notice an increase in synchronicity. Although I have noticed synchronicities in my life for a long time, I am deeply aware now that synchronicity is an outcome of being intimately connected with the universe. With the fixed self gone, the universe flows through. When the universe flows through, ordinary human limits are transcended. All of creation participates in responding to your every request. And why not, since every desire is now an expression of consciousness creating through you!

I have become aware that the soul is nothing but a focal point for this universal flow of consciousness. Before enlightenment, I conceived of the soul as a higher 'self', still fixed somehow, still belonging to 'me'. Now there is no 'me' to belong to, since there is no 'other' to separate from. In experiencing life from the perspective of soul, I see that there is no fixed 'soul', just as there is no fixed 'self'. As the yogis have always said, "Atman is Brahman", the individual soul is not separate from the universal soul, or God. I am not the same as God, but we are not separate. We are two aspects of the same reality.

In this recognition, there is far less resistance to life. It is like being part of a river that sweeps everything in its path as it flows towards its destination. I am no longer pushing it, so it no longer has to push me back. There are times I go back to trying to do things the old way, planning for the future, attempting to direct my life in certain channels. The more I push, the more frustrating it gets, until finally when I give up, the universe begins to reveal its own plan, so exquisitely better than anything I could create by myself!

It was interesting to leave Oneness University, and first notice a newspaper. I have been somewhat of a political and environmental activist, very much aware of all the wrongs in the world, very intent on trying to get people to see the truth. Somehow, I don't feel the need to 'change the world' on the outer level anymore. I can see that all the chaos and human drama is an outcome of a deeper evolutionary push that is forcing us to clean out our closets, and I feel comforted in the knowledge that despite all the evidence of our outer senses, our passage into the Golden Age is assured.

I realize that I am a very beginner on this path. Shortly after my enlightenment, when Grace and I were invited to a 'darshan' with Bhagavan, he told me that at some point, if I choose it, there will come a 'dark night of the soul', where everything will begin to drop away, all the good feelings, all the synchronicities, even the sense of direct communion with God. "You won't even have the ability to create any kind of meaning in your life anymore," he said.

It would be akin to Christ's 40 days of wrestling with Satan in the wilderness, and necessary in order to enter into deeper states of oneness with God. Right now, I am aware of a sweet glow surrounding the enlightened state, but the 'dark night' could literally feel like going through 'hell'. It is a necessary stage if I choose to clean out the unconscious mind, and not everyone may choose to do so. The unconscious mind, says Bhagavan, is my personal link to the Ancient Mind. Having cleaned this out, you literally become a 'Christ'. It is what the ancient initiations in the Great Pyramid were designed to do.

Perhaps this 'dark night' is similar to what the Australian aborigines and shamans in various traditions refer to as 'dismemberment', in which one's entire foundation of being is erased. Everything that has provided meaning in the past disappears. This is a deeper stage, necessary in order to de-clutch from the collective mind of humanity. It is from this state that Jesus was able to effectively realize his mission. It is from this state that the critical mass of enlightened people will be able to move the rest of the world into enlightenment.

I remember sitting in a bookshop one day as a young teenager, drawn to a book which spoke of the descent of the Holy Spirit after Jesus ascended from his physical body. There was a baptism of power, and the disciples were empowered to go out into the world and heal the sick, raise the dead, and cast out demons, just like he had done. "All these things you shall do, and even greater things than these", he said, "because I go unto the Father". Ever afterwards it was all I wanted to do, and prayed that I too might become one of his disciples, that I too would receive this 'baptism of the Holy Spirit'. I remember feeling so disappointed when I was told by well-meaning clergy that the age of miracles had passed away with Jesus, and that these kinds of things were not happening anymore.

Perhaps there is an ebb and flow to all cycles. I have seen that the age of miracles, if it ever really passed away, is once again here in our midst, and I am so grateful to be a tiny instrument in this vast plan for the liberation of all humanity.

There is a new humanity being birthed, a new Earth arising in our midst. I pray that the winds of Creation inspire each of us towards this realization. May we each become an empty sky for the whole universe to blow through!

~~~~~~~~~~ ✸ ~~~~~~~~~~

Bhagavan's Wind

I searched through the world's illusions and strife
For the pearl beyond price, for true meaning in life.
For long years I grappled with right and wrong,
Uncertainties and doubts, as I struggled along.
I read all the books, and in strange postures did bend
Howled through the night for old traumas to end.
I suppressed all my passions, all earthly desire,
Sacrificed all to the Great Cosmic Fire.
Yet through all my struggles it was clear to me
I wasn't any closer where I wanted to be.
Thus I journeyed through life, I gave up my youth,
Grew old with my questing, still searching for Truth.
Until finally one day on my visioning rock
With painful clarity I knew I must stop.
I'd followed each rule, tried only to love,
Given up Earth for Heaven above.
Meditating for years I still could not stop mind,
And deeper cravings were all I could find.
"Could it be", I asked in restless confusion
"That this search for the pearl is itself illusion?"

~~~~~~~~~~ ✸ ~~~~~~~~~~

~~~~~~~~~~ ✸ ~~~~~~~~~~

A dangerous question – the conflict grew worse:
"Could it be that my seeking itself is a curse?"
Too old was I now, too set in mind's ways,
But my seeking was worthless, I saw through my daze.
"Yet to give up the search would surely be death –
So safe in illusion I will draw my last breath."
Then one day I met Bhagavan, and Amma, his wife –
Surely the grandest event of my life!
And suddenly was light, the heavens were riven.
A gold ball descended, the deeksha was given.
"Can a drowning man pull himself out by the hair?
Can mind discover stillness by running here and there?
Seeking brought you here, now the seeking 'self' must die.
Efforts cannot earn you grace, however hard you try!
Mukti avatar am I, come to give mankind this grace –
All ye who yearn for suffering's end – to live in life's embrace."
Gladly I heard the words, and gratefully received.
No longer was I slave to mind, my lifelong conflict ceased.
The seeker died, along with self, the cravings all died too –
No more Wind Rider now, only the Wind blows through!

~~~~~~~~~~ ✸ ~~~~~~~~~~

Part 2

Other Experiences of Enlightenment

13. Grace

In this section I share other people's experiences of enlightenment. When I sent out a call for people to send me their enlightenment experiences I was overwhelmed by the deluge I received. There were enough stories to compile an entire book; however, in the interests of space, I decided there was no way I could include them all. Perhaps there will be a future book based entirely on people's experiences, and I invite readers to contribute to this as you have your own experiences as well. Meanwhile, I have chosen four accounts to share, all of whom I know well. As you will see, each person's experience is quite unique. I begin this section with Grace's experience.

In all the following accounts I have taken the liberty of changing the name 'Kalki', when it has appeared, to 'Bhagavan'. As I have mentioned earlier, it is a name that was given to him, and stuck to him for a period of time, but he feels it has created too many concepts and expectations, and is unwilling to use that name for himself anymore. Where they refer to the 'ashram', I have also changed this to 'abode' or 'Oneness University'. I have also changed the term 'dasaji' to 'guide', which is the term currently used to refer to the carefully trained enlightened assistants living there.

Grace had the privilege of being among the first group of Westerners to get enlightened. Amma's birthday is August 15, which also happens to be India's Independence Day and Sri Aurobindo's birthday. Shortly after this day last year, tens of thousands of people gathered for a darshan with Amma and Bhagavan in Nemam. In the first experiment of this kind, Bhagavan decided to use the occasion to initiate the transfer of enlightenment to people gathered. I will let her speak for herself.

~~~~

How we came to Bhagavan's abode is in itself, grace. Looking back, I see can see his guiding hand over a period of months. One day in April we were having lunch in Auroville when two women sat down beside us, eating a large plate of fruit. They had just come from Oneness University in south India and were filled with glowing enthusiasm about Bhagavan's dharma. We were intrigued, and thought we would perhaps go sometime before I had to leave India.

Shortly afterwards, we received several emails from trusted friends in the US, urging us to attend a healing arts gathering
~~~~

known as the Experience Festival. It was being held at Oneness University. When Kiara investigated, he was invited to speak, and we were both invited to attend. As teachers, we had the honor of meeting Bhagavan in the first few days. I found him pure delight! He was kind and funny and welcoming, yet embodied a deep quiet power and presence that was unmatched in my experience.

Later that week, we attended a Mukti program. Within a couple days of starting the course, we were taken as a group to Nemam for darshan with Amma and Bhagavan in honor of Amma's birthday. There were tens of thousands of people there, and as part of the group from the course, we were blessed to sit in front, where we remained for two darshans. During the first darshan, two male guides were placing their hands on people's heads giving deeksha. I really didn't know what this was all about, but I observed carefully what was happening and felt there was definitely more power coming through one of them. As I observed him something within me said very powerfully, "I'm ready". The guide, who was some distance away, looked at me, caught my eye, and nodded. He immediately changed his course through the crowd as if he had heard me, and was in front of me within a few minutes.

He placed one hand on Kiara's head, and one on mine, pressing firmly for perhaps two or three minutes. I felt like I was being hit by lightning but in slow motion. The heat and electric charge built up until it was almost unbearable. When he took his hand away, I was unable to move or open my eyes for about 40 minutes. Several large bumps appeared on my head that were extremely tender, and my whole head throbbed and buzzed. Luckily they allowed us to stay for another darshan, since I was unable to see or move. When we did leave, we had a bit of lunch there, and then took a taxi back.

I was very disoriented, nauseous with a pounding head and surges of heat everywhere. I was barely able to walk, and totally unable to think. Back in our hut, I went directly to bed, and fell into a deep sleep.

The next morning I awoke to great peacefulness. I felt like a vast still lake. It was not an empty stillness, but very fluid and alive, and filled with a quiet completeness and joy.

That morning before class, I stood in front of the 'srimurti' (portrait) in gratitude and reverence, when Amma and Bhagavan's eyes started to sparkle and move! Amma's eyes began to blink as I looked at her. I was unable to believe what I was seeing and looked around to see if anyone else could see this. I waved to Kiara to come and look, but he did not see me.

As we meditated later, a large opening came in my ajneya chakra, so big, dark and visceral I put my hand up to see if there was something pressing on my forehead. In this opening I suddenly saw myself lying there on the floor, although my form was very different. I was a man with a grey beard dressed in white. I felt great feelings of love and familiarity. I knew this was me without question, and said to myself in wonderment, "Oh! I am really that man!" Later the guide told me that the man was Bhagavan, and the experience was to show me that he and I were one.

The next day in meditation, as we brought energy up through the chakras, it went through my crown and beyond. Several tubes of opalescent light rose from my crown chakra to a flat, elliptical disk some distance above my head. The disc was also a very beautiful diamond-like opalescent color, silvery, golden and pink, and very subtle; a rarefied, highly refined beauty and ethereal vibration.

The disk slowly began to rotate, very serene and beautiful. As it moved, beams of light radiated out from it. Some were large and powerful, others subtle and more fine. The beams spread out across the planet, and I could see the earth from space, a blue marble with an amorphous pink cloud of love fed by these beams, moving and undulating around and over the earth. I walked home feeling like I was this rarified, fine and delicate frequency in human form, my feet barely touching the earth, so light and delicate and beautiful was I.

A little later I saw one of the guides and told him of my experience and that I thought I was seeing a new chakra. He explained that my chakra system had made its link with universal consciousness. He said we were intended to be linked in this way, but had somehow become disconnected. Now that I had been reconnected, he said, I could become enlightened.

That evening we were taken as a group to a darshan with Bhagavan. When we got there, Bhagavan told us "I am going to do something we haven't done with Westerners before. We will be giving everyone the deeksha. Everyone will become enlightened, if not immediately, then within 24 hours, or 48 hours, or over the next few weeks or months. The seed of enlightenment will be planted."

I knew somehow definitively that that it would be 48 hours for me. He explained about putting the guides into a high state of divine union where they would transfer bliss to us. He said not to worry if they got a little noisy; they were simply going into states of ecstasy! And to please keep our eyes closed.

As we sat there, I heard such tremendous laughter and sounds of joy from the dozen or so guides that I opened one eye and peeked as a female guide started giving deeksha to the woman next to me. I thought, "What has he given them?"

The guide was in a very high state of divine ecstasy, trembling and laughing, face skyward, cooing in bliss. Her face was one vast smile and tears of joy were on her cheeks. When she gave deeksha to me, she hugged me, caressed me, and kissed my cheeks. As I touched her, she was like a gentle little faun trembling in my arms.

After her came five or six male guides giving deeksha. None had the impact of the first deeksha in Nemam, but the cumulative effect was immense and overpowering.

I 'cooked' all night, electrical surges of great heat coursing through my body, a splitting headache, great sensitivity to light, and disorientation. This continued all day, and the next, and when it began to diminish that evening, I said, "Bhagavan, you can finish me off, I'm ready!"

Immediately the heat was turned up, and I began to cook in earnest. This continued with increasing intensity through the night and into the next morning. It was Sunday and everyone had left for another darshan in Nemam. The last thing I wanted was another deeksha to the boiling pot within my head! We decided to go to our hut and have a quiet meditation while the group was in darshan. I was feeling so poorly I lay down on the bed.

Then I heard a mighty rumble like a freight train, which came in and around my body. The heat became unbearable, every nerve ending on fire. This freight train energy rumbled up through my physical and subtle bodies, lifting me up off the bed like I was a paper doll. My heart pounding was deafening, my breathing became faster and faster.

As the energy reached my heart, tears flowed silently from my eyes, the joy surged and my face became an immense smile from ear to ear. My neck arched and head went back as the energy shot through my crown and beyond to the 'bliss body'. I went into a state of ecstasy, laughing and laughing uncontrollably, my body being tossed around like a limp rag doll.

During this time I had only two awarenesses. First, "It's happening!" And second, "Thank you Bhagavan".

I saw Bhagavan's face smiling at me through the whole experience. He was right; it was a purely neuro-biological event. Normally a mystic, I saw no wondrous mystical visions, I simply felt and heard the tremendous energy tearing through my body. When the laughing subsided, I had no control of my body. Arms and legs didn't work. I was unable to speak. I was in a place of pure delight with everything.

My husband was watching all this, and gently touched my aura with his fingertip. I shivered and giggled. Every slight touch, movement, or sound was immense. After perhaps an hour and a half, I was able to sit up; looking at him blissfully, as I tentatively touched his nose with my finger and laughed in pure delight. I was looking at the world through the eyes of a baby, pre-verbal, in wonder of everything. Noses are such a source of delight for a little baby, the funniest thing you can imagine!

Simultaneously, I was an immense consciousness, vast, and wise and observing in deep wonder...

Sometime later we were outside. The trees looked endless, and my husband so tall. Eating was interesting with motor skills of a young child; sometimes I missed my mouth completely. At the same time, this vast new presence that was 'I', was everywhere and nowhere.

Kiara called a guide, and he came laughing, saying "She's got it. It is the classical enlightenment". That day I progressed to about two and a half years old, and that night everything became overpowering. Light, sounds and smells were causing me intense pain. Kiara was concerned and consulted a guide, who said "She is going through some sensory changes. By tomorrow she will stabilize".

The next day I felt better, and about 4 years old. Four is a delightful age. Everything is pure delight, an adventure and so much fun! The following day I was 8 years old. That evening we went to see Bhagavan. I felt like a very little girl. I remember when he turned his full attention on me it seemed the whole universe was smiling on me with infinite patience and love, welcoming me. Bhagavan said to me, "We all know each other now, and we are friends. If you ever need me, just call me, and I will come." What a wonderful thing for God to say when you are eight years old, or eighty for that matter!

Next day we had to leave for Bangalore. I was reluctant to go. I liked my little house, my little bed with pink sheets. When we left, the sky looked so big, people seemed so noisy. In India, sometimes buses can be a nightmare, crowded and hot, blaring music. My bus was a blessing, silent and dark, and I had a whole seat to myself. As we drove through villages, I watched through the open window in a state of bliss. Rainbows around all the lights, I was in fairyland or maybe heaven. Perhaps when you are eight, they are the same.

We arrived in Bangalore. I felt I was a small Bhagavan walking around. No more was I 'myself'. Kiara's brother, a genius in computer engineering, asked me a few days later, "What is enlightenment?" I said, "I don't know. I don't know anything, and it's okay." He said with great seriousness, "I think that's what enlightenment is".

Since then I have had eight months of integration, the last three at Oneness University. New peak experiences, new revelations, new ways of seeing the world and relating to people. A steady progression, although, sometimes it seems I fall back. When that happens, it seems to be a gathering up and bringing forward of something deep that needs to be changed. As I begin to observe it - no blame, no guilt, no denial - then it transforms itself, sometimes in a matter of seconds and dissolves into a high state of gratitude and bliss.

Bhagavan says that any emotion truly experienced becomes bliss. This is true. It is our refusal to see something, or our continuing to judge something that we don't want to acknowledge that keeps us stuck and causes us pain. If we just look at it with kindness, and say "oh yes, I see that's there", it goes almost like magic, leaving bliss in its wake. It has done its work, which is to wake us up, so it is free to become bliss too.

I know now what it is like for babies when they are born, when their senses and nervous systems are completely open, how wondrous each perception of their world. How gently and lovingly they must be regarded as they have come fresh from God. Bhagavan tells us that BABIES ARE BORN ENLIGHTENED. (Capitals appeared by themselves as I wrote this!} What does that tell us of the importance of our realizing this as a human species?

This has been the latest of my own personal revelations. I have remembered how I felt when my children were born; not unlike being here with Bhagavan and all these enlightened people. I was in bliss the first 9 months of my daughter's life, and realize now I was truly in the presence of an enlightened being. Until I got caught up in the material world and the rat-race of acquisition we call life in the affluent west, and didn't have time to just be with them. And then our beautiful children forget who they are, just as we did.

Bhagavan has come to return all of us to our natural state, the state of our childhood, the state of enlightenment.

And enlightenment is just the beginning.

14. Barry

Barry Snyder Martin is a close friend who lives in northern California. He and his partner, Karen Anderson, first pointed me toward Bhagavan by forwarding an Experience Festival newsletter, which inspired us to come to Golden City and eventually meet Bhagavan. I then invited them to come to India and experience what was going on here for themselves. Barry and Karen attended a 5-day enlightenment process in March, 2004. I will let Barry report his experience in his own words. What makes this account particularly significant is that he had already had experiences of enlightenment before coming to Oneness University, and so was able to make further distinctions about enlightenment based on his prior experience.

~~~~

The journey with Bhagavan began an eternity ago, when we all came into embodiment to realize the fullness of the Divine here. In this lifetime, I first heard of Bhagavan in 2003, when my partner, Karen, noticed an article about the Experience Festival in the Global Village newsletter. She immediately felt that our dear friend Kiara, who had recently returned to his native India, might be interested in learning more about this upcoming festival.

As it turned out, the Festival was held on the grounds of a man called Bhagavan. Kiara not only became involved in the Festival – he and his wife, Grace, also went to see Bhagavan and attended a deeksha. When Kiara wrote that Grace had become enlightened, I wanted to know more. I began to meditate with Bhagavan's picture, and felt a very high frequency of golden-white light pouring in. I received the strong knowing that experiencing Bhagavan's presence was somehow THE next and final step in my journey of awakening.

I had experienced numerous kundalini awakenings and Oneness experiences, beginning in 1986. I resided in the Oneness most of the time, and yet deeply engraved emotional patterns still sometimes arose, and when they did, the veils of the separated mind would temporarily engulf me. After nearly thirty years of inner work, a number of patterns still remained, and while they grew less powerful over time, they
~~~~

nonetheless continued to be a source of suffering and discontent.

I came to realize that something was amiss in the neurological structure of my physical body, particularly the brain. I did many brain-clearings using numerous inner and outer technologies over the years, yet I never found the switch to turn off the separate ego's periodic control over my consciousness. I knew I had to go to India to see Bhagavan when I read an article in which he said that enlightenment is a biological process, and that he was akin to a surgeon who altered the brain structure and function, resulting in illumination. The lights went on! This was the missing piece I'd been seeking! I immediately made plans to attend the next Enlightenment Process. I could hardly wait to receive the deeksha, which, I had read, changes the brain structure and establishes enlightenment.

Powerful shifts in consciousness began to occur as soon as we arrived. It felt as though I was being worked on by Bhagavan 24/7. The first really powerful experience occurred during the three-day Samskara Shuddi (an emotional clearing process). After a particularly potent catharsis, an energy descended through my crown chakra and I felt the body dissolve.

Soon, the afternoon session was over and everyone got up to leave, but I could not make my body move. There was no place where I could find a connection between personal will and the body. In fact, I couldn't sense any personal will at all, in this state of empty Oneness. As I lay on the floor, there was no fear, just a curious observing of this state, and an unconcerned wondering about whether someone would eventually come and notice me lying there, and whether I might go to the bathroom in my pants if this state lasted indefinitely. These idle wonderings evoked no feelings, other than detached amusement. Whatever happened, it would all be perfectly fine.

After what I would guess to be about 45 minutes, a fly landed on my arm and involuntarily the body decided to move on its own. Instantly it became clear that the body is fully conscious and capable of doing everything it needs to do in order to convey the soul through life. Such a deep letting-go came with this realization! I could relax and let the body do it all.

Then I found the body getting me up into a sitting position. Gradually it decided to walk me out the door to experience the magnificence of the sunlight. I walked out and stepped on the earth as if for the first time. The sensation was ecstatic, delicious, a super-sensuous union with the earth. To this day, the body continues to be orchestrated through a superconscious connection, and I, in a way, am just along for the ride, yet one with all that is unfolding. It is also clear that the body is embedded in all of creation, and thus all of creation is also carrying me in perfection and without effort.

In another Samskara Shuddi session, I became aware of a sense of sadness around the severe damage I had done to my left index finger when I cut it to the bone with a hacksaw in the spring. All the nerves were severed, and had not grown back. I had become resigned to living life with no feeling in the tip of this very important finger. It was annoying when things would slip out of my hand, and I felt sad about the loss of the sensuous connection of touch in caressing myself, others, and the many wonderful things of life.

The moment I embraced the sadness in its fullness, and acknowledged the desire to have it healed, I felt the descent of the presence of Bhagavan, down through the crown chakra and into the arm and finger. Within moments I realized that I had received the majority of feeling back in the finger. Joy, gratitude, and reverence for the love and power of Bhagavan filled my heart, along with an all-encompassing love and the desire to see us all totally happy and joyful. I also realized that I was not able to fully open to this magnificence; thus, the feeling in the finger was not completely restored. But it continues to gain more feeling by the day.

The deeksha was the crown jewel our experience, and the most profound and pivotal event in this lifetime. When Bhagavan arrived, I instantly knew that the spiritual path had come to an end. As I watched him empower the guides, tears of overwhelming gratitude flowed freely. The spiritual power was so great that I had to crawl up to the deeksha line; the ability to walk was gone. When the silver sandals were placed upon my crown chakra, the bliss was overwhelming. With each transmission from the line of guides, a cascade of bliss, love, and joy dissolved all sense of 'me'.

Looking into the eyes of the guides was looking at the only Self that exists. Oneness obliterated all other sensations, along with a complete emptiness that was at the same time a fullness of such love, peace, joy, bliss and happiness that it is not to be described, only to be experienced. Drunk on divine bliss, I staggered away from the deeksha line, waving to everyone as they laughed with joy at my obviously altered 'drunken' state.

Lying on the floor, I felt complete liberation. The heart knew the long search of the ages was over. Such a peace was present – "the peace that passeth all understanding" that they always talked about in church. Now I understood those words – I was experiencing them. The peace was accompanied by immense love and gratitude for Bhagavan. All self-sense was consumed in this state, which continues to grow stronger to this day. The only desire I felt was to deepen endlessly into this state and to devote my life to assisting others to experience it too.

Now, months later, the process continues to deepen, and a profound dissolution of all sense of a separate self has become the main feature of reality. The state of deeksha seems quite solid, while the full-on intensity comes and goes in waves. I've even played with the state to see if it could be short-circuited or shunted. No such possibility. 'No-self' is here to stay. Occasionally there are glimpses of what was before, as the faintest outlines of old mental and emotional habit-patterns briefly reappear. But, like clouds that dissipate before a thunderhead can form, nothing ever comes of them. The basis for suffering and separation seems to have disappeared. Thank God.

Old patterns of reality orientation are gone, too. During the weeks following the deeksha, our sleep cycles and dietary preferences were in a constant state of flux. One day, I'd wake up at 3 am, sleep all afternoon, and go to bed late. The next day, something totally different would unfold. One day Karen slept nearly 24 hours, after sleeping just two hours the night before. The physical body appears to need immense amounts of time and space to integrate the divine infusions. The body gets up and moves when it wants, and when it doesn't, it cannot be moved with an act of mind or will, which seems to have become practically nonexistent. Yet what needs to get done is accomplished without effort or force, easily and efficiently.

There is no sense of disturbance by outer circumstances; events and sensations flow through with grace and ease. Subtle imprints of previous patterns that seemed irresolvable occasionally pass across the screen with no sense of substance, attachment, or other impact on the state of being. They are as ephemeral as clouds traversing the ever-empty sky. The sense of gratitude to Bhagavan is beyond expression. A state long yearned for, intuited as a possibility, is now here – and so much more – and this is just the beginning. It feels as though the journey has just begun.

The only blip on the screen has been that, after returning to America, the mind went back and forth about whether I was enlightened. In the emptiness of being, I knew I was, yet feelings and thoughts of doubt arose from time to time. Whenever I held them in the Bhagavan's consciousness, I heard, Yes, you are enlightened, it is just the mass thought form of doubt passing across the sky of the mind. One morning, in a flash of light, the deeksha energy fully anchored in the heart. Before this, the heart was unsure at some level, not yet fully connected and integrated with the golden ball of light in the head. Now the heart knows – I AM THAT!

I discovered that the heart was under the mis-belief that enlightenment meant perfection – no more "stuff", no more judgments passing across the mind. Now it is clear that enlightenment means awakening to the realization that I AM THAT, and THAT is the supreme light, supreme love, supreme intelligence, supreme truth that Bhagavan is. Bhagavan is the intermediary to bring all of this to mankind! He is the full embodiment of THAT, with the gift of the ability to transmit this realization to mankind. Once it is transmitted, it is done and final. The deeksha is infallible, since it comes from God. Some people do not realize it right away, as the screen of the mind may be too heavily clouded over to see the light of the Supreme One shining through... but is nevertheless there. They have it, but are still hypnotized to some degree, which will surely burn away over time.

Many of us have deep neural grooves which act as attractor patterns for the Ancient Mind net. This results in a continual downloading of stuff from the ancient mind. As soon as those attractors patterns were shut down, and the new attractor pattern was activated which tuned to the higher self, monad, paramatman whatever you want to call it, it was all over. It is as though Source consciousness was now anchored and embedded into the center of the brain, in the

Cave of Brahman. Now none of the clouds of illusion could holographically play within the brain structure.

Today the heart fully knows – I AM THAT. For some days I was aware that Asuras were attempting to distract, confuse and deter the process. They have no power over the Supreme One, and surely the Supreme One is their demise. There is no need to deal with them or even to deal with their effects in this world as they work through the lives of men.

What is left is simply being – beyond time and space, without past or future – with all of creation arising within this empty field of I AM.

15. Mitchell

Grace and I met Mitchell Jay Rabin, and his partner Rena Majeed, shortly after the Experience Festival in February 2004. We immediately, along with Barry and Karen, developed a close friendship. Mitchell lives in New York, and hosts a television show called A Better World, (see **www.abetterworld.net**), dedicated to bringing healing and enlightenment to the planet. Along with Rena, he participated in the 5-day Enlightenment Process from March 1-5, 2004.

~~~~

I had the golden opportunity to meet with Bhagavan and then to conduct an interview for A Better World, an educational TV program in New York of which I have been
~~~~

the host since 1993. Well, this gave me a unique moment in which to get to know this amazing being. The interviews went extremely well – he was relaxed, the embodiment of kindness, warm-hearted and simply a pleasure to be in the presence of. He also wanted to discuss the 'world situation' with me and come up with the solutions to the most agonizing of problems. It was deeply gratifying and soul nourishing to have time with this amazing soul.

Meeting with Bhagavan was in itself a taste of awakening, but the Enlightenment Process was where we really experienced our own 'splendor and fullness of being'. A brief description of the experiences I had from receiving the deeksha would be to say that everything that would have been considered happening 'outside' me was now happening 'inside' me. There was no separation! The lights were turned on! I was in an utterly awakened state. Laughter and crying of others near me were happening inside me.

Funny thing to say, because 'I' was no longer 'I' as I knew I in any ordinary way, but the 'I' I knew in the depth of my bones. It was the 'realest I' going.

We were touched by the hands of a few 'guides', after they had become visibly ecstatic by what appeared to be the simple viewing of Bhagavan and Amma's srimurti (photograph). But who knows really what induces such divine intoxication? All I know is that when they touched me, and sprinkled a few drops of blessed water on our heads, my reality changed. I went through this experience about six times. Truly, half of those were mild shifts, and the other half? Ecstatically poignant.

All experience was direct, totally rich and fluid. There was also no separation between any idea of God, God itself, and 'myself'. I most immediately discovered this when, in the midst of ecstasy in gazing at the sky, I exclaimed, "Thank God for all this!" By thanking God, I was thanking everything equally, including 'myself'. There was no difference. This is when I knew that the Awakened Self was what was present.

It was as though 'the lights simply got turned on'. I was in a reality in which all was One, and this was known totally as in the natural course of things. I felt so alive! Until then, oh I was alive to some extent, and indeed, more alive than many, but now the deeper, higher Self got turned on, and I saw from the place where All was connected... It was like the circuitry was finally completed and I could see and feel reality clearly.

I was in the 'truth-state', in harmony with All. It was the state from which teachings flow forth. For the first time in my life, I felt that I could get rid of all of my 'spiritual' books because now I could speak or write them. To have them would be redundant. I recognized that having them and reading them was a compensation for what I hadn't been in touch with inside myself. And I have compassion for this unawakened condition, God knows! In the awakened state, this whole perception of Life was the book itself.

It was that a part of my brain, dormant by and large until then, got stoked, prodded, awakened by the deeksha. As Bhagavan says, this is a neuro-biological process. I wholly agree. All of our brains and nervous systems are hardly used and are largely dormant. It is always said that we only use 5% of our brains, right? Well, until now. Through this process of deeksha, I now know something more, at least a bit more, about that other 95%. Within it is the treasure trove of ourselves. Not more book-learning, not more concepts, but the domain of "knowing", a place of spontaneous love and insight, of deep seeing, of deep and abiding unconditional brotherly and sisterly love, joy and compassion.

I gained, through the masterful touch of Bhagavan, access to the rest of the brain, the nervous system, indeed my true energy field. He helped me gain access to "myself". But this self isn't 'me' in any ordinary sense. This self was the same self of all beings, if it could be called a 'self' at all and is Divine. To say 'I AM THAT' made inherent, organic sense. My ordinary sense of self was not to be found anywhere. And at the same time, the words of Bhagavan echoed: "6 billion souls, 6 billion different enlightenments".

There remains a distinct personal blueprint, like an individual flower of a species that is now expressing this reality in its own unique way. It was an abiding in peace, of love, of knowing, of presence. Call it God, call it Cosmic Joy! It doesn't matter. It is what it is and it is the stuff of reality that is our true, Divine Self. Tears of gratitude, bowing head in grace, were interspersed with peels of blissful laughter. Such was my experience.

In my life, the ingestion of sacred plants our precious earth offers that are psycho-active, in conjunction with years of Tai Chi practice, Chi Kung, involvement in the Gurdjieff Work and Buddhist and Taoist meditation practices, opened the doors to my consciousness so that the "terrain" I entered from the deeksha was already quite known to me. This was not new territory, but no less wondrous. The sacred drink of the Santo Daime in particular, which originates in the Amazon, seemed to prepare the way well.

I was joyful and humored to see the similarities. Bhagavan said that these dimensions, where the neuro-pathways in the brain have already been cut, would be the first places the deeksha would guide one to and through. So there I was in the middle of south India and I felt that I could as well have been in the jungles of the Amazon! But it was better than that. The light kept shining. There was no toxin or substance in my system. This experience came from an internal source itself. Catalyzed by a frequency 'outside' myself, it awakened one inside.

I was what I was always looking for.

In Golden City, this holy place for which we had spent many lifetimes preparing to come, this humble, still, intent being, Bhagavan, through his guides, touched us, and awakened our consciousness into its appropriate divine place. The dream of lifetimes was coming to fruition. I went to India on an intuition and a hunch. I hadn't been there in 7 years. My visits to other gurus, interesting and worthwhile as it was, didn't 'do it' for me. There was no connection to speak of, and certainly no offer of enlightenment. Here, the power was being given away. Bhagavan says, "Be your own teacher. Take the deeksha; let your own enlightenment guide you. Then, if you want, go back to your own religion or practice or teacher, enlightened!"

These are the words of a Master. He wants nothing but for this beautiful Earth, and all of our playmates, our brothers and sisters, to be in our fullness as divinized, joy-filled beings all the way to the core. You know, when you really look at the biochemistry, you see that the human organism is designed for the ongoing experience of joy, pleasure, and bliss.

What's an endorphin? What are the skin and the senses? A fragrant, yellow-bursting flower? There's no escaping it – we are set up for bliss. But, look at us. We've missed; we've totally missed the mark. We live instead in suffering. These are not new ideas to me, nor possibly to you. But now I'm living the truth of it, it is feeling and experience based. They are not just words. They are my reality.

So all the teachings I've ever listened to are now living in me. They're not static, they're not intellectual, they're not even just a mild stoke. They have a real, living home inside me. I had been leafing through some old writings and came across a journal entry I made years ago. It pleaded with the heavens for enlightenment and the ability to wholly serve, with all my being, this precious planet, people and universe. Similar pleas to the Universe are scattered all throughout my writings since I was around age 15. Then, in one gentle "hit to the head", I was awakened to that reality!

Shakespeare was right, this world is a play. I could see how this state, free from suffering, free from duality, simply 'plugs' a person into the large cosmic picture and everything assumes its rightful place. If everyone were enlightened, there would not be a world of war, of environmental destruction, of 10% owning and controlling 90% of the world's resources – it simply wouldn't happen.

So do I see this process as a means of truly taking this planet to its next level? Enlightened government! Enlightened society! Organic farming! Water distribution! Music! Dance! Fun! No kidding! It's so simple it boggles those committed to the complicated. Unwinding the damage will take a little time and doing, but it is do-able. The vibration of all of us enlightened people will itself be a major force in the un-doing of the imbalance.

How wonderful! I see hope, I see hope, I see hope! As brothers and sisters, we are literally One, and to hurt another is to hurt oneself. This is no longer an idea. When one awakens, it is real. The games of power and control cannot be perpetuated. They lose their power, and there's no lure in this realm. The material realm is joyous, but it is not a realm any longer of 'power over' but 'power with'. From the view of Golden City, and my view being there, this is the way it is.

The world as we've constructed it, with all its rights and wrongs, institutions with regulations, God in religions with rules, social restrictions, military might, all look mighty strange from this view. Where did we get so many odd ideas? And why did we institutionalize them all? Soon we'll all be free!

With this feeling in my breast, with all of us feeling this, the world will be transformed. There is no question about it. The power of reality, of truth, will assert itself. It is happening, right now. It is so powerful. There are powers at play far beyond anything we now know. Like a major ripple effect, 100th monkey style, with the first few thousands enlightened, the rest of humanity will open like flowers. And the world as we know it today, with the wars, with the environmental destruction, with human pillage, will cease to be. It will simply cease to be.

Let it also be known that the peak of deeksha shifts. It does not remain in full regalia. What follows remains beautiful There is a permanent shift in the energy field and the shift in one's perceptions can be called upon by being witness, observing the drama of daily living, and while being wholly in it, also watch it. And the flower-opening of humanity will be upon us in no time. Thank you dear Bhagavan & Amma, for catalyzing in me my truest Self and empowering me to serve sentient beings in a higher way. Blessings to all!

16. Freddy

Freddy Nielsen was the first Westerner to discover Bhagavan, and the first to bring this message of oneness into Europe. He had come to India seeking the non-dual state of enlightenment more than a decade ago, and was led to meet Bhagavan through an extraordinary series of circumstances. We got to know him during the Experience Festival in August 2003, and were deeply touched by his simplicity, kindness, and passionate dedication to sharing Bhagavan's message with the world. He received his enlightenment in June 2004. Below are excerpts from his early experiences as shared on his website **www.livinginjoy.com.**

~~~~
~~~~

I am in the middle of a very special process in Golden City. Many of you may know me personally or indirectly, and I felt I had to share some of the totally incredible things that have happened this last week…It was the 14th of June…I was hit in the head by an immensely strong Light, and then I got the most unbelievable experience of my life…

I saw there was nothing but an immense explosion of bliss and love. This was life, and there had never been anything apart from this. I merged with this eternal fountain of bliss, which people are calling the Spirit, the Supreme Power or simply God. But it was not the Supreme Power, for there was nothing but this Power, so how could it be Supreme when there was nothing to compare with? I slowly began to explode inside this immense Bliss, and it was the power of billions of atom bombs. How I survived, I still do not know. It must be by Grace. I got so many tremendous revelations about the entire Universe, I can write several books on these 5-6 hours.

After some time I had to go to the toilet. I could not move because of the intensity of ecstatic bliss, so I don't know how I managed to walk these 5 meters. I told Bhagavan (He was fully alive within me) that this was the intensity of 100 orgasms. Immediately the bliss-energy got explosive and I told: Sorry Bhagavan, it is even 1000 times stronger. Again the energy was increased manifold, and I had to agree that this was like a cosmic orgasm 10 000 times stronger than a human one…No words can ever describe it. It is billions of times more beautiful than anything in this world…

On the 16th at around 4 pm I was suddenly given one more deeksha. What happened can never be comprehended by the mind. It was as if Bhagavan showed me billions of universes after having repaired my brain completely. All bad files were deleted. The ego was very big, and Bhagavan was jokingly trying to remove it in a serious manner, but realized it could only be uprooted with some very powerful instruments... I felt as if Mike Tyson had given me 10 minutes of a series of knockouts after I had drunk 2 liters of Vodka. I was completely helpless, and Bhagavan showed me I was nothing, I could understand absolutely nothing. My ego had to surrender. I felt that my ego was less important than the smallest dust particle in a remote galaxy.

Then my guide came and told me to open my eyes, he said that my ego was dead and that there was nothing but Bliss and One Reality. He added that I was that bliss and that there had never been a moment when I was not enlightened. It was all an illusion that Bhagavan had removed from me. I opened my eyes and looked at the Philips tube light in my room. I felt millions of volts of eternal bliss flowing out from my eyes (but there was no ego left, I had become everything).

Whatever I looked at gave an eternal explosion of bliss inside the body and the eyes, even much deeper than the 10 000 times cosmic orgasm two days earlier. Now it was 100 000 times stronger, not just 10 000 times. This was the power that could destroy hundreds of galaxies in seconds and I still do not understand how this body survived!!! It must be that Amma and Bhagavan are very skilful surgeons.

Then whatever I listened too also became an incredible explosion of bliss and love. I even screamed at times, for the body had difficulties in handling the immense explosion. One of the guides came and congratulated me that I had finally "made it". I felt so much love for him that I exploded, and I think I must have squeezed his hands very strongly. I had little or no control. All was immensely explosive and ecstatic bliss and love. Any sound gave immense ecstasy, and I became the sounds. There was no ego; I became everything I experienced...

~~~~

Today is the 20th of June, and it is 4 days ago I got the divine operation of the brain...

There is no limited person called Freddy anymore. It feels as if he was an illusion that lived billions of years ago. But the memories are there, and these memories can be compared to a wave. So I (or better to say "consciousness" or simply "the eternal ecstatic explosion of love and bliss") am sometimes inside the wave when I have to be functional. But most of the time I am all that I experience.

I am the wind caressing this body, I am the mountains or stars that I see, the sounds of people or nature. I am one with everything. I am everywhere, yet nowhere. I am God, yet I do not exist. I am everything and nothing at the same time. I feel bigger than the entire universe and smaller than an ant. In short, there is nothing to understand for me, and I do not know who I am, or if I am, there is only an immensely powerful explosion of bliss and love, and there is nothing apart from this. Sometimes I am that explosion, sometimes I am consciousness looking at this explosion.

The most common experience when I sit down and look at something is that I am empty, and God is looking at God. Freddy is forever gone, and there is only the Power, the Spirit.
~~~~

The Totality experiences itself, and it happens inside the sensory organs when I am in body consciousness. And the great thing is that I can play tennis and football very well in this state, and it feels like the only natural thing in the Universe.

All else is a dream, an illusion. There are maybe 2 hours a day when the energy is not exploding with the power of 10-100 orgasm experiences throughout the universe (this is my average state), and that one could call the dull state. For a person still having the illusory self left, the dull state is called "depression". For me, the dull state can be described by this: I am happy, feel eternal peace and there is absolutely no suffering.

I met Bhagavan yesterday for the first time after he and Amma operated on me, making my entire nervous system in harmony with All That Is, with the Universe. I cried out of gratitude and it was soooo difficult to speak... I could cry out of gratitude and fill an entire ocean with my tears, and that would be showing less than one millionth of my gratitude, reverence and love for him and what he is doing...

~~~~

I got two more deekshas, one the 25th and another one yesterday the 28th. The results are totally amazing and next to impossible to describe. The deeksha the 25th was so powerful that the other 2 previous ones look quite small. A completely new dimension of experience. For 3 hours I was in billions of places simultaneously and was the One Supreme Spirit, and there was total oneness with It (God). My old life of having a separate existence was blown away in a few hours, and there is only oneness now.
~~~~

All is automatic and I am not the doer. All actions are done, they simply happen just like the wind does not decide where to blow. In the outer life I look ordinary, doing all what I did before. But before I was the one who did things, spoke, wrote, ate, etc. Now there is no center within me who can decide or do. It is simply done, as if the entire Universe does it, and not I. And that is the greatest of all freedoms. Each experience is natural, and I feel a bit like a newborn blissful baby experiencing everything for the first time. All is fresh, all is new, all is total.

One week ago, there was a small remnant of the separate Freddy wanting to merge more with the eternal ecstasy and love I felt pulled into. There was a hidden fear that this may go one day. But now there is no such feeling, there is no one to check or control, not an inch of separation from All That Is. It is so beautiful that the love and joy almost kills me...

During the earlier deekshas I felt that I was sometimes the wave but felt union with the sea. My tremendous love and bliss was felt from outside, entering into my field of experience. Now I have totally become united with all Life, and I am the experience. This is called as Aham Brahmasmin in India, "I am All That Is, I am Brahman". But I feel it is much more, for I am that, and at the same time the Spirit beyond all Creation, what we call God. So "I am Brahman" means totally being Nirvana or Tao. And apart from that I feel the Power that created all this, and It is sooo real, that I am drunk in its Presence all the time, from the point of being Life itself...

I am the happiest child in this world. All is immensely alive, fascinating and touches my heart so deeply. The gratitude is bursting from within. But God only knows who feels grateful to whom. It is as if The Supreme Spirit has swallowed me up intensely, all the time experiences Itself through all my experiences, all that I see and hear.

Yesterday's deeksha deepened it all, and it became so natural to live in this new state. As if my life had always been like this only. I am as much you as I am the thoughts that come. Your actions are as much mine as are my own actions. No ownership within. For practical purposes, the body and mind continue to work as before, as if I am a separate person, but it has in fact nothing to do with me. After the deeksha yesterday, I lay down in the garden. I could lie like this for an eternity. Nothing has to be done, I am everywhere, and all is perfect...

There is only God, only One Reality, nothing else. Only one single wave that we call life. No one owns life, it is not mine or yours, there exists only LIFE, and nothing but that. And we are all that One Life, and there has never been any separation. All that is a mere illusion, popularly called Maya in India, Samskara by Buddha....

All galaxies and the entire Creation are inside my body, I feel it clearly, as if I am the Source of all life. Love explodes like billions of volcanoes, and there is only Light, and I am that Supreme Light. I feel as if I am dead once and for all, and when you die, Life swallows you and let you experience at times as if you are the source of all. It is like having all the ecstatic bliss and joy in all worlds inside your body... Amma and Bhagavan are 100% alive inside me and it is them who give all these states to me, and I love them beyond any description and thank them immensely.

~~~~~~~~~~ ✸ ~~~~~~~~~~

Empty vessel

Was there ever a longing
That is empty of truth?
Is the bee ever drawn
To a nectarless flower?
Then why bang my head on walls?
I have identified with the "seeker"
When all that I am
Is a vessel to be emptied!
I am so full of myself,
Pictures, expectations, longings –
What happens if I surrender it all?
True surrender is an act of grace,
surrendering even the need to surrender.
In letting go I am already filled.
In giving up control,
Every dream I have ever had
Finds its home.
So hard yet so easy,
It takes a million to realize
That it only takes an instant.
I've hit bottom in the bottomless pit of desire.
I am ready for you now, beloved Friend.

~~~~~~~~~~ ✸ ~~~~~~~~~~

Part 3

Collective Journey of Enlightenment

17. Mukti Avatars

Who is this man who is having such an extraordinary impact upon the world? Who is Amma, his wife? Were they born avatars? When did Bhagavan first become aware of his mission? And Amma of hers? How do they propose to enlighten the world? What are the limits of their capabilities?

I had often imagined what it would have been like to know someone like Jesus personally, to walk with him, to witness his miracles, and to be able to ask him these questions. Little did I know that I would one day be led to the Golden City and witness a revolution in human consciousness perhaps unparalleled in our entire human history!

Who is Bhagavan? The term means different things to different people. "Anyone in India can call himself a Bhagavan," he says humorously, "and there is no need for controversy around this."

He does acknowledge himself as an Avatar, however. "An avatar comes to Earth in response to humanity's call. He comes when there is a certain level of stagnation, and he comes with a specialized mission. An avatar is the descent of higher consciousness. It need not necessarily be a spiritual being. For instance, Gandhi was an avatar of non-violence, and Einstein was an avatar of physics. Any higher consciousness taking birth can be called an avatar." He refers to himself as the Avatar of Enlightenment. His mission is to give enlightenment to the world.

Many consider Bhagavan to be a 'Poorna Avatar', a total embodiment of divinity. Throughout the ages, avatars have descended to kindle the forces of enlightenment in a few people, but Bhagavan's mission is to kindle a collective manifestation of divinity in the mass consciousness of the planet. I believe that Bhagavan is not just an individual, but also a collective consciousness, the same consciousness that is known variously as Christ consciousness, Buddha consciousness, or Unified consciousness.

Bhagavan was born on March 7, 1949 in a village in Tamil Nadu called Natham. He was given the name Vijay Kumar. Ever since he was a young child of two or three he has been aware that he was a descent of divinity here on Earth to serve humanity. He tells of how his parents would take him to the temple when he was young and circumambulate around the images of various gods and goddesses. All of a sudden he would find himself inside these images and have to stop moving. People would ask him why he was not moving and he would say, "I am inside this god looking out, how can I move around myself?"

He did not experience suffering and was always in a very happy state. At first he thought everybody was like him, but when he saw that they were only experiencing suffering he realized that his job was to bring them out of suffering. This knowing was very deep within him already at the age of 4 or 5.

One of the games played by the village children was where they would enact some of the ancient stories. He was always chosen to play Krishna or one of the gods, and would be asked various boons, and they were always granted. Even the elders of the village would come up to him and put some grains in his hand, and he would bless the grain and they would have good crops.

It was at age 9 or so that the golden ball began to appear to him. He realized it could be used to send into people and help them to awaken, but he was not able to activate it at first. After working with it for a long time certain chants would come to him, and as he chanted these words, it would begin to activate. He continued working with this golden ball through adulthood, experimenting in many ways to see how it could be used to help people.

When he was 28 or so some mutual friends introduced him to his future wife, Padmavati, now known as Amma. She was born on August 15, 1954 in a village called Sangam. She was a mystic and would go into deep states of samadhi from early childhood. She too was deeply concerned for humanity, and felt that she was here to liberate people from suffering. From the time she was little, she let her parents and childhood friends know that she would only marry God, and would know him when she saw him. Strange as they thought this was, they accepted this.

When they were introduced to each other, they immediately recognized each other and knew that they were meant to be together and work together. She had first seen him in a statue in a temple, and knew that soon she would be meeting him. Her childhood dream was fulfilled. Their marriage took place on June 9, 1976.

Amma had already become quite well known for her mystic powers, and her ability to grant boons and perform miracles. She was regarded in her village as an aspect of the Divine Mother. When she left her village the entire village became sad. They felt a divine power leave the village.

There is a story that when some villagers first saw her picture taken along with Bhagavan they became furious. How dare this man sit beside her! They eventually reconciled themselves to the idea that since she said she would marry God that this must be God. So that was how it began for many of the villagers!

There was a time when Bhagavan was the director of a school in Andhra Pradesh known as Jeevashram. He realized that many of our social ills stemmed from a faulty educational system, and was interested in helping to create a new model of education that concerned itself with the flowering of the heart as well as the intellect.

It was during this time that the miracle of enlightenment first happened. Bhagavan had always known that he was able to help people in various ways, grant them boons, heal their illnesses, and so on, but he wasn't able to liberate them yet. One day his son, Krishna came bounding into the classroom very excitedly saying that a golden ball had entered into him, and was causing him to experience all kinds of wonderful states of consciousness.

"All right," said Bhagavan very composedly, "see if you can pass it on to someone else." So he passed it on to another classmate of his and she had the same experience of being able to enter into cosmic consciousness and experience all these other 'lokas', or dimensions. Many students from this school chose to help Bhagavan in his mission, and are now disciples and active members of Oneness University.

This was back in 1989, and was the beginning of Bhagavan's experiments with giving enlightenment to people. It quickly spread like wildfire. Many students started experiencing these enlightened states and all kinds of strange things started happening. They could make the winds start and stop, they could make the rains come and go, they could enter into other times and lokas, they could enter in and out of pictures, and they could heal people with a touch. Not only that, people simply walking or driving by the road outside Jeevashram were also beginning to spontaneously experience all kinds of mystical phenomena.

But soon the parents began to get upset. "What is happening to my child", they wondered. Bhagavan realized he would have to take it slower, and withdrew these powers.

Eventually, at the repeated requests of his students he agreed to create an order of disciples, with the only requirement being that they joined with their parents' permission and blessing.

This order of disciples has grown over the years and now numbers about 180 members/guides. During the first few years of the order, Bhagavan was still not very sure about giving enlightenment to the masses. This shifted in the middle of 2003. Up until that time he did not know for certain whether this grand experiment of global enlightenment would succeed in time to avert global catastrophe. After this point, it felt like something had shifted, and he knew with absolute certainty now that his mission would succeed, and that humanity would make it. We were divinely destined to successfully move into the Golden Age, and mass enlightenment could now take place.

With the first guides, the deeksha was given directly by Bhagavan himself. The work was still very experimental, and the results were not always predictable. Some of these first guides went into non-functional states of nirvikalpa samadhi for months. It was a blissful divine state, but not very useful as far as actively working in the world.

Gradually, he was able to modify it so that a person could experience high states of samadhi and still remain functional in the world. As he continued experimenting with the transfer of power coming through him and acting upon the neurobiological circuits in the brain to create the conditions for enlightenment, he realized at a certain point that anyone, and everyone, was capable of becoming enlightened. It was only after this realization that he began his work with the masses, for he didn't want anybody to feel that they were incapable of receiving it.

Many of the first guides had been experiencing cosmic states of consciousness over the years that he had been working with them. Few of them, however, had attained the permanent state of enlightenment. In June 2003, Bhagavan called them together, and had them go through 42 days of intense sadhana, during which he personally gave them deeksha. Each of them became enlightened.

As the work proceeded, the power of the deeksha grew. In the early stages, he would have people go through 18 months on a 'fruit only' diet to heighten the sensitivity of their subtle bodies. This is no longer necessary now. He found that what was taking 18 months to prepare for was now taking two months, and then three weeks, and then ten days. He began training the enlightened guides to do the deekshas themselves. As they attuned to his consciousness, and transferred the golden ball to others, he was able to follow the energy of the deekshas and do the necessary work of surgery. In later phases, he found that he was able to do this entirely from a distance.

It was after this that the floodgates of enlightenment began to open. He now began to give deeksha to larger groups of people, both Indian and Western. The first public deekshas for enlightenment were given on the occasion of Amma's birthday, on August 17, 2003. A few days later, the first weeklong deeksha course was given for Westerners. Grace and I were among this group.

At this same time he also started giving deeksha to masses of Indian devotees, including entire villages. Many hundreds began coming every day from all over the country for one-day programs – a short teaching followed by a deeksha – which has now been extended to 6-day programs.

In early 2004, longer courses started being offered to lay people from all over the world Several 10 day courses were offered, along with even more profound 21-day courses designed to take people into the state of oneness deeply enough so that they themselves could transfer the deeksha of enlightenment to others. Many all over the world have now been prepared to give this deeksha. A continually updated list of deeksha givers can be accessed on the websites listed in the back of this book.

The work is continuing in leaps and bounds. Every time one person receives enlightenment, it makes it easier for everybody else. Since Amma's birthday on August 15, 2004, not only is the power of the mukti deekshas continuing to grow but an entirely new phenomenon has begun. Known as the 'phala deeksha', this process is designed to put participants into a state where they can directly meet Amma and Bhagavan in their cosmic body, and ask them to fulfill whatever desires they may have, whether it is for health, enlightenment, finances, or other circumstances in life.

Unlike ascetic notions of God found in various religious traditions, Amma and Bhagavan believe that material realities have a valid place on the spiritual journey. After all, will a person whose sole concern is for survival have the energy required to seek after enlightenment? The difference between their two approaches is a matter of degree. Amma tends to be somewhat more focused on speedily granting people their wishes. Bhagavan's focus tends to be on first getting people enlightened.

The next stage of Bhagavan's program for mass enlightenment is the completion of the 'Oneness Temple' being built at the Golden City. This temple has been designed using a form of ancient Vedic sacred geometry known as 'vaasthu', and will serve as a physical anchor for the next stage of Bhagavan's work. Sacred geometrical proportions utilized in the Mayan and Egyptian pyramids have also been incorporated into the design.

The plan is to have upto 8,000 enlightened people meditating in it at any given time, creating a strong morphogenetic field of enlightenment, and transmitting this state directly into the mass consciousness of humanity. It will be completed towards the end of 2005. It is expected that once this is completed, Bhagavan's ability to transfer states of enlightenment to the masses will increase exponentially. People will simply have to walk through this field in order to experience a witness state, which is the first stage of enlightenment.

As the power of the deeksha grows around the world through the increasing number of people who are being trained as deeksha-givers, Bhagavan emphasizes that it is very important that it should adapt to the local culture and religion. There is nothing intrinsically Hindu about enlightenment. If he were born in China, he says, the same work would have a Taoist flavor; if he were born in the West, it would have a Christian flavor; if he were born in the Middle East it would have a Muslim or Jewish flavor; for a growing minority of people around the world who consider themselves outside any religious boxes, it would have a metaphysical or universal flavor.

We need to be extremely sensitive that as the work proceeds in different parts of the world, or even here in India, that it not become a religion or a cult. From the perspective of cosmic union, it makes no difference whether the gift of enlightenment comes through Bhagavan or Christ or White Buffalo Woman or Allah or Krishna or Inanna or Buddha, or whatever image of deity or wholeness one believes in.

"You can have a picture of Jesus on the altar and give the deeksha, and the results will be the same," he emphasizes. Organized religions, when used to divide people, usually cause more harm than good, and the last thing he wants to do is to create yet another religion. Once our guiding light comes from within, all religions will die a natural death, he predicts.

Bhagavan expects once the critical mass of people is achieved, it will only be a matter of a few months before the rest of humanity becomes entrained to the increasingly strong morphogenetic fields of the enlightened state. There will be a moment when a doorway between the worlds opens, and humanity will step through this doorway collectively as an enlightened species.

I am told that Bhagavan is only manifesting a tiny fraction of his power at this time, some say only one percent. He could turn up the volume to 100% any time he chooses, but it needs to proceed in stages. He recognizes that to unleash too much shakti at once could be painful and destructive, and so he is holding himself back. As the work grows, and the morphogenetic field of enlightenment gets stronger, more and more of his power will be revealed, until all structures of human separation will collapse in the face of this rising tide.

It is expected that as the strength of these morphogenetic fields continues to grow, more and more people will begin to move into permanent states of enlightenment with just a single deeksha. Soon, it will become possible for anyone who has received deeksha to give deeksha to anyone else and give them enlightenment as well. Eventually, the individual deeksha will not be required anymore.

The state will be transferred through a glance, through a touch, through a prayer. It will happen through dance, music, and art. It will happen as people in the healing professions go about their daily work. It will happen as people fall in love. It will happen as people open their hearts and eyes to suffering humanity. It will happen spontaneously as an unstoppable tide of grace coursing through our collective consciousness.

Already, spontaneous combustive awakenings are beginning to happen all over the world. Perhaps the morphogenetic field is already strong enough for those whose souls are ready. It is a feedback loop. The more people that become enlightened, the stronger the morphogenetic fields of enlightenment become. This in turn causes the DNA of the human species to positively mutate, which then modifies our nervous systems to naturally receive enlightenment.

In the years to come, spiritual seeking and striving may become totally unnecessary, and ultimately counter-productive. A state of gentle, relaxed openness may be more effective, as we open ourselves to an evolutionary force that is so much bigger than anything we know. What is coming is truly unimaginable and will not easily fit into the spiritual and intellectual boxes we have defined for ourselves. All teachings and practices will become irrelevant as the power of this wave sweeps through our collective being.

Bhagavan is clear that this is the age of the collective avatar. The new cosmic creation emerging in our midst is too vast to be manifested through a single embodiment. He is a major point of descent for the Supreme One, but ultimately it will descend everywhere, through everyone. His mission is to prepare the way so that all of us together, as a group avataric force, become the architects of a new cosmic cycle. Once this happens, he says, his own work will be done!

This is not a passive event, but a co-creative act. As we become collectively enlightened, we become this avataric force. It will be an order of enlightenment far beyond anything we are now able to experience as separate enlightened individuals. The human family will begin to experience itself as one global entity, one rainbow of many colors, one planetary self with many pairs of eyes, one planetary brain composed of 6 billion central nervous systems!

What this will look like in the years and decades to come is beyond our wildest imaginings. This will be the new dawn so many have long awaited in every age and tradition. This will be the day when the gates of eternity will be opened to all, and God's dream will be realized. Or perhaps it does not yet exist even in the mind of God, and is being dreamed into existence, co-creatively, moment by moment. This is why Bhagavan has taken incarnation. This is why we have taken incarnation. These are truly the times we are born for!

A new dawn

First streaks of dawn,
The twinkling lights of an age gone by
Fade into eternity past.
I wake up shivering
From my illusions of sleep.
Why must darkness precede the dawn?
Why is death the prelude to birth?
No matter;
The long night is ended now.
The first rays of a new dawn
Illuminate my path,
Beckoning me to follow.
Can I shape the coming day?

18. Miracles

I have not focused very much on miracles in this book, because to put too much of a focus on them would take away from the greatest miracle of all, the profound gift of enlightenment that so many are beginning to receive. Still, miracles of healing, divine grace during moments of crisis, and even instances of people being raised from the dead are becoming increasingly commonplace.

The most commonplace, of course, is physical healing. Numerous healings are being reported not only during the mukti programs, where incredibly high cosmic energies are being transmitted through the guides, but also at Amma's darshans in Nemam, and in the privacy of people's homes in response to prayers.

Our bodies are designed for health, and there is a divine intelligence within us, which knows exactly how to create health and dispel disease. This intelligence gets freed up when kundalini is awakened, and healings happen. Physical healings are a direct outcome of natural law. Miracles are simply a manifestation of these laws, and perhaps someday physics and medicine will find a way to address them within the context of these natural laws!

Since a lot of kundalini gets activated during the mukti programs, many healings take place during these events. These programs typically attract a lot of people, usually several hundred at a time. There seems to be a critical mass of two or three hundred people at which point spontaneous healings often happen. I have heard of repeated instances where the blind began to see, the lame began to walk, the deaf began to hear, and various forms of terminal illnesses began to clear up. Many of these have been written up in 'Krupa Darshan', the official magazine for the Golden Age Foundation. A book, *Miracles of Sri Amma and Bhagavan*, has also been published by them, a compilation of miracles experienced by many people around the world.

The physical presence of Bhagavan and Amma is not required for these healings to take place. Many devotees have established their avataric presence so deeply within their 'antaryamin', the sacred abode of divinity within their own heart, that miracles often take place for them in response to faith.

In one such story, there was a man whose doctors had told him that he would need a kidney transplant. He was walking down the street one day, slowly and in great pain, when an old man walking behind him poked him sharply with a stick directly over one of the weak kidneys. When he looked back, the old man simply grinned at him and winked. Irritated, the devotee continued walking down the street. Suddenly, he felt another sharp pain in his other kidney, and again looked back to see the old man grinning at him. The devotee scolded the old man, who then walked away.

Meanwhile, as he continued to walk along, he noticed that a huge crowd had gathered around. There had been a terrible road accident, and the victim was being carried away on a stretcher. He was deeply affected, but didn't dwell on it any further until his doctors, examining him the following day, pronounced in great consternation, that his kidneys were completely cured. Wearing the disguise of the old man, his 'antaryamin' Bhagavan had performed a kidney transplant for him, using the healthy kidneys of the accident victim.

I have heard several such stories from people, about how the 'antaryamin' Bhagavan or the 'antaryamin' Amma would physically manifest for their devotees in response to crisis, or even in response to devotion. In one instance, I am told of a devotee couple who maintain a room in their house for Bhagavan and Amma. They put a new bed sheet down every night, two glasses of water on the bedside, and the required toiletries in the bathroom. Every morning, the sheets are crumpled, the bathroom has obviously been used, and the glasses of water empty!

The boundaries between the physical world and the mystical world are very thin. These boundaries disappear in the enlightened state, or in response to faith. As my guide said to me once, "the self is the dividing line between the physical and mystical worlds". When the 'self' is gone, such events become commonplace.

I have heard of numerous instances where Amma or Bhagavan appear to their devotees in physical form, then disappear into the 'srimurthi' on their altar, or where they receive a phone call from one of them in response to urgent need, or where an incredible series of synchronicities takes place in response to a prayer. The physical Amma and Bhagavan may not even necessarily be aware that these miracles are taking place!

In one instance, a friend of mine from Sweden, Mattias, reports how Bhagavan gave him a valuable teaching. One night, in the middle of a cold Swedish winter, he had driven his car up a remote, curving, mountain road. Having reached the top, he got out to breathe in the clean air, and take in the night sky. He was feeling a deep gratitude, and oneness with everything.

After he got back in the car, he impulsively said to Bhagavan, "Show me what I would be like without God". He then started to drive downhill, very slowly because it was icy and slippery. After a couple hundred meters, for no apparent reason, the car suddenly flipped around 180 degrees, with only the snow bank to keep it from plunging down the cliffside. It was impossible to move the car. Shoveling didn't help, nor anything else he could think of.

Half an hour later, soaking with sweat, and freezing, he realized there was nothing else he could do. There was little hope of someone coming to help, and with the gas tank on reserve, he knew he couldn't keep the car running for warmth. He came to the conclusion that if he stayed in the car all night he would likely freeze to death, and figured that his best chance of survival was walking 5 to 10 km to the nearest house.

He told Bhagavan, "If you don't help me I will have to go since I can't do anything else". Just as he was getting ready to walk, he heard a voice, "Don't be a fool, just drive the car". In that moment he felt the whole car being lifted and moved 180 degrees around. Amazed, and thanking Bhagavan for the valuable lesson, he drove away!

Another story refers to a plague of locusts in a certain village that were destroying all the crops. One farmer prayed to Bhagavan for help, and suddenly a huge swarm of birds appeared, ate up all the locusts in his field, and only in his field, then disappeared. When asked about this later, Bhagavan remarked that these birds had come from another dimension, or 'loka'. The veils between the lokas was quite thin, he explained, and anyone could perform miracles if they had a strong relationship with their 'antaryamin', and were able to stand between the worlds and hold a strong intention for such a thing to happen.

Just as the power of the deekshas continues to grow, so does the power of these miracles. There is an amazing phenomenon taking place in a village in Orissa, one of the eastern Indian states. A woman was healed of a terminal illness when she came to Amma's darshan at Nemam. Afterwards, she would light a ceremonial lamp on her altar, and apply the oil to her body. She applied this same oil to friends and family members, who started experiencing cures for their own illnesses.

The power of this healing oil has continued to expand, and today there are tens of thousands of people a day from all the neighboring villages and towns making their way to her doorstep. Bhagavan says that he is allowing this to continue as an experiment. He realizes that if the collective human consciousness is confronted with change too quickly, there could be a massive backlash. If opposing forces do not try and stop this work, these kinds of miracles and healing phenomena will spontaneously start happening in more and more places around the world. Just recently I hear that another such phenomenon has broken out in the state of Andhra Pradesh. Such outbreaks of miraculous healings are expected to increase around the world.

In another recent phenomenon, a devotee looked up at the full moon one night, and was shocked to see the faces of Amma and Bhagavan clearly superimposed over it. He started telling other people, and soon thousands were observing the same phenomenon in awe. This continued until sunrise the following day.

There is one story I particularly like, because it very clearly reveals the natural balance between human consciousness and the environment. Bhagavan shared the following account in one of our darshans with him.

One day, people from a certain village came to him and said, "Bhagavan, we want rains". He made a few enquiries and came to know that these men drank regularly and beat their women regularly. So he said to them, "Look, if you stop all this, I will certainly give rains". The villagers countered saying, "Bhagavan, first you give rains and then we will stop beating our wives".

Bhagavan relented. He gave them rains, and they had a good crop. They earned more money, so they drank more, and beat up their women more. "So this year there have been no rains there, and I said I am not going to help you out this time!"

"So here we see how human relationships and mother earth are related", continued Bhagavan. "If relationships are breaking down and there is no love in the community, this affects the weather. Once relationships are set right, rains will come. So we have to work on our own consciousness and that will help Mother Earth to revive herself. She is sick. This is how we can help Her. Ultimately it all boils down to becoming enlightened, which means becoming free of the self. The self is a curse. It has to go."

Just as the consciousness of matter can directly be affected through the influx of divine intent, so the consciousness of the Earth is intimately connected with the thoughts and intents of collective humanity. Many scientists and mystics have been talking about the distinct possibility of massive earth changes in years to come. Bhagavan himself has said that unless human consciousness undergoes a rapid change, there will be widespread devastation on the Earth. Can we take our God-given birthright as planetary citizens to change this?

I will end this chapter with one such example from my own life. Even though this took place well before I met Bhagavan, it illustrates the connection between human consciousness and Earth events in a way that is particularly important for us to understand today as we move into the cataclysmic possibilities of the next few years.

I was in Berkeley, California during the September 1989 earthquake. Shortly afterwards, many psychics and 'sensitives' in the area were picking up the likelihood of a much bigger earthquake to come, one that many had earlier predicted would be 'the big one', washing large parts of the California coastline into the sea. One well-known shaman was receiving detailed visions of what this would look like, and was even given a very specific date for when the earthquake would happen.

Thousands of people began to focus their prayers and energies towards transmuting this probability. The night before the due date, many of us felt something had suddenly shifted. The following morning, as I turned the radio on, I heard that the Berlin wall had come down at the exact time that my shaman friend had 'seen' for the big earthquake! Somehow, our collective prayers and intentions had indeed 'brought the walls down', but in a very different way!

Bhagavan tells us that the probabilities of cataclysmic earth changes can be completely averted if there are enough enlightened people anchoring the state of unified consciousness in various trouble spots on the planet. May we take our responsibility seriously as caretakers for the Earth. May we become channels for the greatest miracle of healing we can give to Her – the complete restoration of our home planet to a state of unparalleled, pristine beauty!

19. Summary of Teachings

Having shared something about the journey itself, and a little bit about the global mission that Amma and Bhagavan are here to accomplish, perhaps it is time to highlight some of Bhagavan's teachings.

First of all, what is enlightenment? Bhagavan defines it differently in different contexts. For a neurologist it is the shutting down of certain parts of the parietal lobe. For a biologist it is a slowing down of the senses. For a psychologist, it is loss of the ego. For the philosopher it is becoming a witness to life. For someone on a spiritual path, it is about opening your heart to life, and developing the capacity to love.

When asked to define love, Bhagavan says that he can only tell you what love is not. It is not about neurotically possessing another person. It is not based in neediness or attachment or fear of loss. It is not a justification to control somebody's life. What most people call love is not love, he emphasizes. To experience love you require a mutation in your physical brain. Only then can you experience the love of a Buddha or a Christ. No amount of spiritual or psychological effort can take you there.

Enlightenment is to be free from the sense of separate existence, he emphasizes. The sense of a fixed identity disappears. Once you become enlightened, what exists is only the other. You experience oneness with all creation, and eventually oneness with God. You experience the gift of being human. You experience what it means to give and receive love.

In the realization of this oneness, there is joy. As long as the self exists, it can experience pleasure, but not joy. When things are going your way, you experience pleasure; when things are not, you experience pain. But this is very different from the causeless joy of pure being where you are no longer separate from any aspect of creation or creator, no matter what the circumstances of life.

Bhagavan says that the next best thing to enlightenment is knowing that you are not enlightened. This is not a frivolous statement. "Don't pretend to be enlightened if you are not", he affirms. Many of us on a spiritual path have built up a spiritual persona around ourselves that is as difficult to break through as any of the darker expressions of the mind, and perhaps more so.

The main obstacle to enlightenment is not in the particular quality of the self-identity that we create, whether it is coarse or refined, material or spiritual, but in our degree of attachment to that identity. We assume that our journey towards enlightenment is a linear progression, and that we can become better and better people until someday we cross the finish line and we're there.

It is perhaps easier for a simple person to get enlightened whose head is empty of concepts than someone who has walked for years on a spiritual path and has all kinds of concepts and expectations about what enlightenment is or should be, or what she is or should be. Ironically, the more attached we become to a spiritual persona, the more we develop a spiritual ego, and the further we get from the enlightened state. The mind delights in creating an 'as if' image of the enlightened self. Now it can continue its game of comparison and judgment, except on a more sophisticated level.

Being good does not threaten its survival, as long as we are simultaneously disowning the bad; being spiritual is fine as long as we continue judging ourselves or others for not matching up to our neurotic expectations. We take the dim radiance of our divinity that still manages to shine through the thick layers of the mind, and enshrine it with religiosity, stifle it with morality, distort it with self-righteousness, and destroy it with spiritual egoism.

I am not implying that it isn't desirable to strive towards morality, goodness, and love. There is a reason that religions exist, and many people have been enabled by being on the spiritual or psychological path to refine or even transform their ego. As a spiritual teacher and psychotherapist, I have seen the power of meditation, and of techniques such as holotropic breathwork, psychosynthesis, regression therapies, and bodywork, to begin to heal the traumas of the past and polish the rough edges of our personality.

If refining and clearing the mind is our quest, then by all means we must continue doing everything that we can in this direction. However, if enlightenment is our quest, we cannot get there by trying to develop enlightened qualities. We need to come to an understanding of the very nature of the mind.

In the courses offered at Oneness University, the first few days are about becoming aware of the prison of our mind. It isn't about trying to change any of it, because you cannot. You are simply witnessing the reality of your mind as it is, the emotional charge, the habit patterns, the assumptions, the traumas, the conditioning, and the masks that we build up in order to survive. As you witness, you begin to strip down the social and spiritual personas, and you begin to understand the nature of mind. You become aware that enlightenment is simply about 'de-clutching' from the mind.

We need to be clear that enlightenment does not mean changing the contents of the mind or getting rid of the mind. To become de-clutched from the mind means that you recognize the mind for what it is, which then no longer has power to make your decisions for you. It is not about becoming mindless, but rather about becoming what the Buddhists call 'mindful', being present with reality as it is.

Most of us feel identified with the mind, but we are not the mind. The mind can be a very useful tool, however.

Enlightenment isn't about escaping from the mind, as many people believe, but simply 'de-clutching' from it. After enlightenment, you find that you are no longer controlled by the mind, and can de-clutch from it when it is not needed. When the mind is needed, however, consciousness comes through and uses the mind with a sharpness, clarity, and versatility not possible before.

To be de-clutched from the mind is to lose the sense of 'self' as a fixed, separate, continuous entity which we refer to as 'I'. Enlightenment is the realization that there is no self to get enlightened. We cannot change the nature of the mind. The mind is simply the mind, but after enlightenment, our relationship with the mind changes. We no longer become enslaved by the content and conditioning of the mind. Thoughts may still come and go, emotions may still come and go, but we recognize that they are not 'our' thoughts or emotions any more. In this recognition we experience freedom.

Bhagavan teaches that there is no such thing as a personal mind. Yes, we have individual thoughts, but they are simply emanations from what he calls the Ancient Mind, a collective 'thoughtsphere' of humanity that has existed from the beginnings of our current civilization, perhaps 11 or 12 thousand years ago. All our fears, inadequacies, turmoil and pain, all our lusts, addictions, insecurities and greed, all our hatred, rage, jealousies and judgments, belong to this thoughtsphere. Additionally, many of our impulses for kindness, beauty, pleasure, happiness and courage also exist within this thoughtsphere.

Our brain can be visualized as a radio receiving station that picks up these frequencies at random, depending on our state of mind or health, physical environment, or various astrological factors. Our own individual traumas or conditioning from the past also contribute to the band of frequencies that we select.

However, our thoughts are not our own thoughts. Because our brain is programmed for separation, we receive these thoughts, feelings, impressions, and emotions as if they were our own, thereby separating us even more effectively from the rest of humanity, which we perceive to be better than, less than, or somehow different from us.

We watch a movie on the screen and very quickly get lost in the illusion that it is real. However, if we slow it down so that we can see it frame by frame, we realize that it is only a movie. In exactly the same manner, we are conditioned by the self to perceive our own life as a living movie.

Enlightenment creates a fine-tuning of the senses where we realize that the sense of a fixed continuous self is an illusion generated by the neurological circuitry of our brain. There is a continual dance of personalities, but no fixed or continuous self that somehow remains the same from birth to death. Consciousness flows through your body moment by moment, but it is the same consciousness that flows through all creation.

When there is no self, there is no craving or attachment. Cravings and attachments are based on a sense of separate existence, or self-importance, where you continually desire things you do not have, or have what you do not desire. When there is no separate self, attachments and cravings cease. When cravings and attachments cease, there is no suffering.

We are not talking about physical or psychological suffering here, but existential suffering. Existential suffering is the incessant desire to be experiencing something other than what is. It is not our pain that causes us suffering, but our resistance to that pain. It is our attempts to escape from suffering that cause us suffering!

Enlightenment means to experience the reality of each moment as it comes your way, without needing to resist it or change it in any way. Once you are willing to fully experience what is there, you are no longer separate from reality. You experience the truth of each moment directly as it is. You become freed from the interference and conditioning imposed by the mind. You experience the causeless joy of being!

You still have mental pathways of old habits, memory and personality, but you are no longer a solid thing. The self becomes porous, and the winds of eternity become capable of blowing through freshly in every moment. You are no longer a fixed 'person' but a dance of 'personalities' blowing in and out of awareness. You are not even a witness separate from yourself, watching things blowing in the wind. You are the wind.

You may still have likes and dislikes, emotions may still come up, but there is no charge left, and as soon as they come up they will likewise go away, just like an infant throwing a tantrum one moment, and staring in wonderment at a little tiny caterpillar the next. There may still be emotional habit patterns imprinted in the body, but these too subside over time.

Another realization that comes after enlightenment is that your body is not your body. Most of the functions of the body are involuntary, but you realize that even the functions that you think were voluntary are not really yours to control. During an enlightenment experience, many people report that their body goes through all sorts of involuntary postures and movements, tears and laughter, completely independent of personal will. It may also become totally immobile, and you realize that there is nothing you can do to make it move, unless it chooses to.

Your relationship with your body changes. You no longer identify with it as yours; rather it simply becomes a beautiful vehicle for consciousness to use. You understand how privileged you are to have this lovely, living body as a means to express the Divine in the world. Each taste, each smell, each sound, each vision, each touch is exquisite, and is as if you are experiencing it for the first time. Each thought, likewise, comes with its own living freshness directly from the consciousness of each moment, an experience that the Zen Buddhists refer to as 'beginner's mind'!

Enlightenment begins with the ability to witness all these things. As you move into deeper states of unity and God-realization, you discover that you have become one with all creation, and that indeed the sense of your own body embraces all of creation. Eventually you discover that you have become one with the Creator as well as creation. You realize, in the words of Jesus two thousand years ago, that "I and the Father are One".

In a nutshell, Bhagavan teaches that:

1. There is only one Mind – the Ancient Mind. It is conditioned by separation and duality.

2. **Your mind is not your mind,** but an extension of this Ancient Mind.
3. Similarly, **your thoughts are not your own thoughts,** but downloaded from the 'thoughtsphere' associated with this Ancient Mind.
4. The sense of a separate self is an illusion generated by the neurobiological structure of the human brain.
5. This 'self', in experiencing itself as separate, generates cravings, aversions, comparisons and judgments, which are the core of suffering.
6. When the self disappears, suffering ends. When cravings drop away, including the craving for enlightenment, you are enlightened.
7. When the 'deeksha' is given, a neurobiological process begins, which leads to the dissolution of the sense of a separate, or fixed, self.
8. When the fixed self disappears, you experience yourself as simply a dance of personalities continually arising and passing away in a sea of consciousness. Underneath all these forms, you experience yourself one with all these is as Atman.
9. **Your body is not your body.** When the self disappears, your sense of ownership of the body disappears, and you experience it as a vehicle for the divine dance of consciousness. Eventually, all creation becomes your body.
10. The mind, based in duality, cannot be enlightened.
11. The self, which is an illusion, cannot be enlightened. **The self is only a concept.** Enlightenment is the realization that there is no self to become enlightened!

20. Deeksha and the Brain

Enlightenment is the ability to see reality as it is, without the layers of interference and interpretation imposed by the mind. It is a simple neurobiological event, and can happen in an instant. Paradoxically, in the moment of your enlightenment, you also discover that you have always already been enlightened! It is our natural state!

The bio-circuitry of a human being was designed in such a way that after developing a self at around age 3 we would return naturally to a state of unified existence at around age 18. Unfortunately, something went awry, and we experienced a Fall within our evolution as a biological species.

Nature demanded that there always be a select few throughout our subsequent history who maintained this morphogenetic field of the natural enlightened state. Historical figures such as the Buddha, Lao Tzu, Jesus, and many others exemplified this. Now, however, we have come to a time when humanity is once again being prepared to return to our natural state as a collective species. The time has come now for each of us to be restored to our natural enlightened state!

Enlightenment has nothing to do with how long you have been on a spiritual path, nor with what your religious beliefs are. You do not even need to believe in God or have any concepts about the soul. Enlightenment does not depend on knowing the right teachings or mantras. It has nothing to do with how many lifetimes you have meditated, or even with how 'good' a person you are.

There is nothing you can 'do' to get enlightened. Enlightenment cannot be achieved through your own efforts any more than a drowning person can yank himself out by his own hair. We are in a prison of the mind, and the key is on the other side. The mind cannot deactivate itself. It can only happen by grace.

Humanity is ready now, says Bhagavan. Each of us has spent lifetimes preparing for this. We have all done our sadhana, or whatever we thought was required, and it is time now to enter the Golden Age together. The question is not if we will get enlightened, but when.

"There is a simple way to know if you are enlightened," my guide had told me once. "If you are asking the question, you are not." The biggest obstacle to enlightenment is to pretend that you already are if you are not.

If you know you are not enlightened, and you become aware of the cravings and aversions generated by the illusion of self, then you become open to grace. When you see clearly the nature of the mind, and the extent of your conditioning, and when you become tired of the resulting suffering – all the incessant comparing, judging, efforting, and blaming – then grace can begin to flow in. Understanding this as a mental concept isn't enough. It must be felt and experienced.

The means that Bhagavan has set up for this grace to act is known as the 'deeksha'. The deeksha is a transfer of power, and can be defined as 'initiation'. It usually consists of a ceremony in which one or more of the 'guides' at Oneness University place their hands upon your head in a state of divine union, and become channels for cosmic energies directed by Bhagavan to reorganize your neuro-circuitry.

Bhagavan refers to this process as 'divine surgery'. A golden ball of divine grace descends through the crown chakra, and the kundalini channels get activated. Certain areas in the brain get shut down, other areas get energized, initiating a process in which the entire brain and nervous system is reorganized (see appendices 2 and 3).

This golden ball is programmed by Bhagavan to reorganize the biological circuitry of the brain, leading to enlightenment. It has a living intelligence, and operates differently within each person. Once it has descended into the crown chakra, however, the process will move towards completion, programmed by the divine 'sankalpa', or intent, of Amma and Bhagavan.

The deeksha punches through the wall of concepts set up by the mind. The winds of heaven can then blow through. In the words of Carlos Castaneda, we open up to the world of the 'nagual', our 'assemblage point' shifts, and we are free.

In the current species of humanity, the brain is designed in such a way as to serve as a receptor station for a certain band of frequencies corresponding to the Ancient Mind. The deeksha serves to loosen up the receptor sites within the brain from this band of frequencies, and simultaneously to dissolve the feedback loops of consciousness that create the sense of separate identity which we have referred to as the self. The brain then becomes sensitive to a wide range of frequencies emanating within the Universal Mind.

To be enlightened is to access our souls directly, rather than through the interference of the mind. Unfortunately, for many people on the spiritual path, even though we have had direct experience of our souls from time to time, our conception of the soul is not very different from our conception of self. It is a 'higher' self, but it is still a separate fixed self. This conception can be a limitation, which is why Bhagavan doesn't speak much about the soul.

The enlightened yogis of ancient India, when they spoke of their inner divinity as the 'Atman', understood that there was no such thing as a fixed individual soul. The individual is holographically related to the whole. The Atman is one in essence with 'Brahman', the universal field of consciousness that is constantly moving through each expression of creation. "Tat twam asi", say the yogis, "I am all of That"!

What happens when the deeksha is given? Some may immediately go into a peak experience of bliss, deep silence, or cosmic consciousness. This may or may not be permanent. If it isn't, this first peak experience is followed by other peak experiences over the following days and weeks, until a permanent enlightened state establishes itself.

For others, there may not be an immediate felt response, and it may take hours, days, or weeks before they start noticing a change. Regardless, once the deeksha is received, the seed of enlightenment has been planted, and Bhagavan will work with you in accordance with your own soul's purpose and the readiness of your physical body to bring the seed into fruition.

The first thing that often comes up for people is an acute sensitivity to the nature of mind, and the patterns that have ruled our lives so long. It can be a shocking and painful experience when we first begin to look at it, but necessary if we are to break free. If more than one deeksha is given, often the first deeksha is programmed to pinpoint the self-centeredness of the mind. If a person has done some self-examination and emotional clearing beforehand, or already 'hit bottom', that can help. Grace only flows when you recognize your illusions. As long as you think you can make it on your own, its flow will be impeded.

Once the deeksha is given, you neither have the power to stop the process in any way nor to help it along. The activity of the deeksha has nothing to do with how deserving you think yourself to be, or with any concepts of spirituality you may be holding, or with making any kinds of efforts towards it.

As Bhagavan puts it, once the train pulls out from the station, will you get to your destination any faster by constantly running around back and forth inside the train? Please realize that enlightenment has nothing to do with the mind or the contents of the mind. It has everything to do with the brain, and the deeksha is an intelligent force which is programmed to do whatever is necessary to create the neurobiological shift necessary to get there!

Many people, after they receive the deeksha, still feel that somehow they can help the process along by doing the right meditations, thinking the right thoughts, or somehow bringing the mind under control. Other people get obsessed with fears about blocking the process through their doubts, fears, or feelings of unworthiness. It is important to realize that there is nothing you can do either to help or to obstruct the process, except simply to witness the process itself.

In other words, if a 'blocked' personality shows up, simply step back and watch the way it works. There might be a fear that you will be the last person on Earth to become enlightened, that you have too many mental blocks, that your heart isn't open enough, that you haven't done enough emotional clearing, that there is something wrong with you physically, that you are too old, too unworthy, too traumatized, or whatever your own personal story might be.

Just watch this personality as if you were watching a movie. Notice how attached it is to the drama of its own suffering. Notice how it sustains itself through its traumas and dramas, even the drama of planning its own enlightenment. Notice how it feeds itself by pretending to hate itself. Notice how its idea of being blocked itself becomes the block. Notice how it wants to analyze itself to death before it is ready to surrender. Notice how it hears only what it wants to hear so it can forever prove itself right.

You may want to make a list of these escape routes of the mind. Give these 'negative' personalities a voice, and describe in detail all the fears, doubts, blocks, manipulations, denials, and dysfunctional habit patterns that you can think of. Then let it all go. Once it is down on paper you may find that they no longer have as much power over you. Once you can see clearly, the seeing itself is the liberation. Once you realize that there is nothing you can do to change yourself, then surrender can happen, and grace can flow.

For some people, even the act of surrender is associated with a great effort. Well, then, surrender even your efforts to surrender. Simply ask for grace and then be silent. Once this 'you' who is so intent on understanding, changing, or healing itself surrenders, enlightenment can happen easily. The neurological shift takes place and you return to your natural state of oneness. It is as simple as that.

It is important to understand what enlightenment is not. It is not about losing your mind, or even changing the nature of your mind. The same mind continues to exist, although you notice that you now have a different relationship with it. Nor is enlightenment equated with cosmic bliss, instant clairvoyant abilities, or high spiritual states. All these may accompany or follow enlightenment at some point, but it is not what enlightenment is about. Enlightenment is simply 'throwing a switch' in the neurobiological structures of your brain, and thereby dissolving the sense of a separate self. It is not about changing the contents of the mind, but seeing the mind for what it is. In this very seeing, all conflict and suffering dissolves, and you experience freedom.

The difference is primarily internal. An enlightened person can still make mistakes, still experience disappointments, still have difficulty with relationships, still experience limitations, and still be bad tempered, except that he will no longer be identified with these characteristics. It is not required that an enlightened person will always have a radiant aura or always be cheerful.

In fact, there will be times when an enlightened person will need to exhibit anger where she would normally be a doormat, or do something quite contrary to an established social or moral code because he is no longer bound by the conditioned identities and learned responses of the old order. An enlightened person discovers joy in being true to himself. He finds no need to pretend anymore, although to an unenlightened consciousness he or she might well be perceived as a rebel or a troublemaker!

Enlightenment is to peel off the layers of interpretation from a given event. To the enlightened person, life becomes a very ordinary thing. You walk, and you are walking. You eat, and you are eating. Enlightenment is not about having extraordinary experiences so much as recognizing that each ordinary moment is extraordinary in itself. Before, there were a thousand interpretations in the mind for everything you experienced. Now, there is only the experience.

It is also important to distinguish between enlightenment experiences and the state of enlightenment. Enlightenment experiences are peak experiences or high energy experiences.

You may go into a peak experience after a deeksha. You may already have had several peak experiences through the course of your life. The kundalini energies within your body rise up to the top of the head, unite with the cosmic energies, and you experience bliss, unconditional love, or cosmic consciousness. You may see celestial visions, even journey into higher 'lokas', or heavenly realms.

Peak experiences cannot be sustained beyond a few hours or at most a few days. The cosmic energies coursing through your nervous system would burn you out and short-circuit the human body, at least in our current level of human evolution. An enlightened state, on the other hand, is permanent. It is a shift in the neurobiological pathways of the brain, resulting in the sharpening of the senses, and the subsequent loss of a fixated self. After a deeksha, there will often be a sequence of one or more peak experiences, which will eventually stabilize into enlightenment as a permanent state.

This can be illustrated in the form of a graph. Supposing the unenlightened person operates from a minus 2 or 3 or 4, depending on their level of suffering. When the deeksha is given, it will catapult them into a plus 3 or 4, where they may have all sorts of phenomenon associated with unity consciousness. This peak experience will not last long, and after a few hours, the experiences will subside. However, once they have experienced an enlightened state, they will not generally dip below the zero-point of suffering. They may stabilize at 1 or 2. During the next deeksha, they may go up to 4 or 5, and then stabilize at 2 or 3. The stabilizing point is higher with each successive peak experience.

21. Deeper into Enlightenment

There is an assumption that once you are enlightened you will never experience sadness, grief, anger, jealousy, or pain, that somehow you have overcome all negative thoughts or emotions. This is far from the truth. The nature of the mind is unchanged.The contents of the mind may also remain unchanged. But without the self to dictate terms, or to differentiate so obsessively between right and wrong, you experience that the 'charge' begins to disappear. You are established in a state of 'witnessing', where the emotional charge disappears. It is a continually deepening process.

Many people associate enlightenment with tremendous states of cosmic consciousness, clairvoyant perception, omniscience, and so on. All these may or may not be associated with the state, but should not be mistaken for enlightenment. Enlightenment itself is a very simple event, and is simply the dissolution of the sense of separateness. It is the natural state in which your body is designed to be.

To become enlightened is to be comfortable with the flow of life. If you are feeling sad, you are not trying to talk yourself out of it. If you are feeling happy, you are not trying to hold on to that feeling. Everything simply is what it is, without the additional charge or carryover from past associations, traumas and conditioned patterns intruding on the experience of each moment. You become fully present with each emotion, each experience. You find, as the guides are fond of reminding people, that every emotion, when fully experienced, becomes bliss.

Each person's enlightenment is unique. Bhagavan says that if there are 6 billion people on Earth, there will be 6 billion kinds of enlightenment. Each person's enlightenment will incorporate qualities of their own soul's desires and purpose. As you progress, you may discover a natural gift for healing, or a great capacity for wisdom, or a deep caring for Earth and humanity. You may experience a deep inner silence, or an all-pervading joy, or a state of oneness with all creation. These states may come and go, and vary from person to person, but there is one thing every enlightened person will experience in common. When the self disappears, suffering ends.

You will still have desires, but they won't turn into cravings. You will still have resistances, but they won't turn into aversions. You will still have a personality, but it will be a fluid dance of momentary personalities that come and go. As you deepen into the state, you will not feel the need to hold on to resentments, fears, and traumas, any more than you feel the need to hold on to good times and spiritual highs.

As you deepen into your enlightened state, there will be continually deeper states of oneness, peace, stillness, love and joy. You will find yourself more and more at home in the mystical realms, and also, paradoxically in the physical realms.

At first, however, the mind might throw up all kinds of conflicts, resistance, and doubt. It is the nature of the self to resist change, and this has become a memory pattern within the mind. This may well come up with great force as the mind tries to deny the experience. As you simply allow this to be, eventually a great peace will descend.

Anything fully experienced is joy. If this one thing were fully understood, your path to enlightenment would be very short indeed. Conflict fully experienced is joy. Pain fully experienced is joy. Sadness fully experienced is joy. Doubt fully experienced is joy. Anger fully experienced is joy. Happiness fully experienced is joy. Love fully experienced is joy.

When the self disappears, our need to constantly make interpretations about reality disappears with it. When interpretations about reality disappear, we experience reality for what it is, rather than what we would like it to be. Rather than constantly craving for what we define as pleasurable experiences, and constantly resisting what we define as unpleasurable experiences, we simply become the experience, moment to moment, of consciousness expressing itself through us.

Enlightenment is both an event and a process. The event corresponds with the dissolution of the sense of a separate self. Beyond this, however, there is a continually deepening process of oneness.

Moving into oneness is not all bliss. At some point you should expect to go through the 'dark night of the soul'. This is a period of profound existential emptiness where the contents of the personal unconscious get completely cleaned out. It could be accompanied by feelings of intense loneliness, heaviness, doubt, or despair.

The 'dark night' is not suffering in a psychological sense. Psychological suffering involves the 'self', and once the 'self' disappears, so does the suffering. The journey into existential emptiness would be impossible if there were still a sense of personal identity left. Rather, it is like Jesus wrestling with 'Satan' in the wilderness, where he cleared out his personal unconscious in preparation for his ministry, or his journey into the realms of hell after his crucifixion, where he was able to clear out aspects of the collective unconscious of humanity.

Not very much can be said about this journey, since it will be unique for each individual. It cannot be lengthened or shortened. It is a necessary part of coming into mastery. Bhagavan says that eventually each of us will have to undergo this experience. As we go through this individually, it is possible that it will clear out the collective unconscious of humanity to such an extent that it will then become very easy for collective enlightenment to happen.

In the more immediate context, Bhagavan refers to three stages of enlightenment – the ability to simply witness life as you de-clutch from the mind, recognition of the inter-connectedness of life, and finally, cosmic oneness. The first stage is when the interference of the mind stops, and your senses come alive. There is the experience of a deep inner silence, and you begin to experience reality as it is. This is what most people will experience after first receiving the deeksha, once you stabilize following the peak experience. It becomes your new sense of ordinary reality.

You might also begin to experience a sense of inter-connectedness with your immediate world – with nature, and with others in the human family. Synchronicities abound and you discover that there is an underlying unity running through all life. This is the second stage.

In the third stage, you have moved beyond the sense of inter-connectedness to complete union with the cosmos. One moment you are a bird, then a grasshopper, then the emptiness of the sky. Here you experience your identity as All There Is. You are everything and nothing. "Aham Brahmasmi", said the ancient mystics of India, "I am this whole process called the universe!"

The experience of oneness with the universe is known as 'samadhi'. At first this experience of samadhi may be very fleeting. In order to hold this experience, every nerve cell in the physical and subtle bodies becomes infused with kundalini energy, and it may take some time for the body to integrate these heightened frequencies.

There may even be occasions when the person appears to 'die' for short periods of time, as the functions of the body become short-circuited. In the early stages of enlightenment, a person may experience peak states of samadhi, but this will not last long. As you progress, you experience increasingly longer states of cosmic communion interspersed by 'ordinary' reality.

The ancient yogis describe four stages of samadhi. The first stage is known as 'savikalpa samadhi'. There is the experience of oneness with the universe, vibrant bliss, and an activation of the subtle senses. Various inner gifts and abilities may open up. This downpour of new energy is refreshingly ecstatic, but can be quite overwhelming to the nervous system, which eventually returns to a more operational frequency. This is the peak state many people experience when they first experience the deeksha.

As the nervous system becomes adjusted to the heightened flow of kundalini moving through the body, it eventually becomes ready for the next stage of samadhi, known as 'nirvikalpa samadhi'. Here the consciousness gets drawn upwards into a unified state of consciousness, while the physical body goes through an extreme shift. Remaining for hours or even days in catatonic states resembling death, every cell of the body becomes transfused with light. This is a relatively non-functional state, however.

Eventually, you move to the third stage of samadhi, called sahaj samadhi. The nadis and cells of the physical body have now become accustomed to the heightened frequencies of enlightenment, and it is possible to live in the permanent state of unified awareness while being fully functional in daily life.

Bhagavan remarks that the enlightenment he gives is intended to be fully functional, and is therefore attempting to modify the nervous system so that people require less time in 'nirvikalpa samadhi' and move sooner into 'sahaj samadhi'. This is the state that Masters such as Jesus operated from. It also requires that the unconscious mind be completely cleared, and the adept may consequently go through a prolonged 'dark night of the soul' before this state is permanently anchored.

A fourth stage of samadhi has been relatively rare in human history. Known as 'soruba samadhi', the physical body is now so infused with higher energies that it has literally become a body of light. The mind is now in complete service to the soul, and the adept is now capable of bodily experiencing any dimension of space and time. This stage is sometimes known as 'ascension', and is the state that ascended masters such as Babaji, Kuthumi, and St. Germaine exhibit.

These masters have chosen to remain close to the Earth dimensions in order to assist humanity, and still appear in physical bodies when needed. There are also many stories of siddha masters in south India, as well as Tibetan adepts, who have taken the 'rainbow body', and simply disappeared in a flash of light. Ramalinga Swami was a well known example of this from the past century. The work of Sri Aurobindo and the Mother was also related to this.

An avatar's job is to make possible what hasn't been possible before. The world is a dream in the mind of God, and an avatar's job, as a divine incarnation, is to exhibit certain states of consciousness in order to open up the same possibilities for the rest of humanity. This is what Bhagavan's mission is. Over time, as more and more people experience these possibilities within their own bodies, it will lead to a mutation within the genetic structure of the human species. For readers familiar with the metaphor of the 'hundredth monkey', this is the potential that Bhagavan sees for humanity as we prepare for collective enlightenment.

All consciousness is a field. The Mind is a field. The Enlightened State is also a field. Rupert Sheldrake, a British biologist, referred to these fields of consciousness as 'morphogenetic fields', or 'form-generating fields'. These are the fields that have shaped our evolution, shaped our memories, shaped our biological forms. Every time one of these morphogenetic fields gets reinforced, it gets stronger. Every time someone 'unplugs' from these fields, it gets weaker.

What this amounts to is that every time one more person unplugs from the matrix of the mind, the Ancient Mind becomes weaker. Every time another person becomes enlightened, the morphogenetic fields of Enlightenment become stronger, making it easier for everybody else to also become enlightened. These two fields are in a 'see-saw' relationship with each other. Soon will come a time when critical mass will be reached, swinging the entire human consciousness into the state of enlightenment. Once this happens, a new species of humanity will emerge.

There is a very interesting study done by an American psychologist, David Hawkins, who has written a fascinating book, *Power vs. Force* on this theme. Using the science of 'kinesiology', he devised a 'consciousness scale' going from 0 to 1000. On the bottom end of the scale were highly charged emotions such as guilt, shame, terror, and rage, and their corresponding states of consciousness. On the upper end of the scale were love, joy, and various states of enlightenment.

Hawkins discovered that one person who was vibrating at the higher end of this scale could offset thousands, even millions of people, who were vibrating at the lower end of this scale. He also affirmed that one Avatar vibrating at 1000 could offset an entire Planetary Mind hell-bent on extinction!

I certainly believe that Amma and Bhagavan vibrate at 1000, or at least very close to it. It is based on this principle of resonant fields that Bhagavan says mass enlightenment can happen. When a person becomes enlightened, their consciousness makes a huge leap on this consciousness scale, which directly affects all consciousness in the surrounding area. When the numbers of enlightened people reaches a critical point, the morphogenetic field of Enlightenment will counterbalance the morphogenetic field of the Ancient Mind, making it possible for a mass enlightenment to take place within the matter of a few months.

There is nothing in life I can think of that is more exciting or meaningful than this!

~~~~~~~~~~ ✸ ~~~~~~~~~~

Long dark night

Desolate winds howl in icy winter night.
The pilgrim stops in his endless wanderings,
And lends his own voice to the wind.
How can it be when the sky is emptied
When nothing remains to obscure the sun,
That life is strangely fed in this mystic darkness?
The silent vastness ebbs and flows.
These riches can only be seen
By one whose eyes are empty of seeing,
When the fires of desolation
Have flared up, then died away,
When the last embers of hope and certainty
Have faded in the night.
How can it be, my Friend,
That I hear you so clearly now
When everything I have ever known
Has smoldered away with these embers?
The storms of separation have passed,
Only the wet snow bears witness.
The dark night is revealed
As doorway to deepest light.
I have found my voice
In the softly running, silent living,
Wild pulsing heart
Of Eternity!

~~~~~~~~~~ ✸ ~~~~~~~~~~

22 .Vision of the Golden Age

The question I had always asked myself was, are we birthing a Golden Age, or are we spiraling into extinction? It would be no exaggeration to state that if we look only at the outer physical realities, we are in extreme global crisis. Where does hope lie for our planet?

Near the beginning of the 20th century the great Indian freedom fighter and yogi-sage, Sri Aurobindo, began to express a truth which had not been expressed before. In his high states of divine union he saw that the time had come for a new stage in the evolution of mankind. He saw that the divine was to manifest right here on Earth and that the time for this divine emergence into Earth life was now. He spoke of heaven descending to Earth, even as Earth experienced a breakdown due to the intrinsic resistance held within her material body towards this 'descent'.

Sri Aurobindo was joined in Pondicherry, India, by a French mystic, Mirra Alfassa, who later became known as the Mother. Together they embarked on a journey of intensive cellular transformation that is very relevant to Bhagavan's mission of Planetary Enlightenment.

Grace and I had spent a fair bit of time in Auroville, the international city founded on the vision of Sri Aurobindo and the Mother. Like Amma and Bhagavan, they too perceived themselves to be a single avataric consciousness in two bodies. They considered their own mission to be that of bringing what they called the 'supramental force' down to the level of physical matter.

Bhagavan himself acknowledges "the incomparable work of Sri Aurobindo and the Mother", and says that without their efforts, his own mission would not be possible. Interestingly, Amma's birthday is the same as Sri Aurobindo's birthday, and Bhagavan and the Mother are both Pisces! Sri Aurobindo left his body shortly after Bhagavan was born. Was he waiting to pass the torch along to Bhagavan before he died?

What is this supramental force that Sri Aurobindo and the Mother talk about? What is it that they accomplished? As I speak about their accomplishment, I am now speaking not from their writings or their teachings, which can be accessed very easily elsewhere, but from what I sense in my own body after my experience of cosmic consciousness.

Sri Aurobindo refers to this supramental force as a divine energy that is descending down into physical matter. Most people think of matter as the ultimate expression of the field of duality, as if divine consciousness was at one end of the spectrum and physical consciousness was at the very bottom. Divine consciousness is somehow considered to be a unified field, while matter exists in separation consciousness. We tend to think of ourselves as separate individuals in the field of matter.

The equations of quantum physics inform us that what we call matter is mostly empty space. They inform us that the foundation of all matter in the universe is a sub-atomic particle known as the quark. In fact, some theoretical physicists go as far to claim that the entire universe is but a single quark continually replicating itself in parallel dimensions of space and time. All matter is related, therefore, they claim, and the appearance of the separate existence of matter is simply an illusion of perception.

It is not matter that is illusion, as many spiritual seekers wrongly believe, but our perception of matter that is illusion! Quantum mechanics has nothing to do with how small a world we are talking about. It is the size of our consciousness that counts, which alone determines whether we live by clear-cut, consensus-based Newtonian laws or an infinite range of quantum possibilities.

How do you translate the richness of these holographic quantum possibilities into a tasteless, senseless, language based world of linear mind in linear time? I had an experience of this once when I was swimming in Hawaii with a mother and baby humpback, and was taken inside her consciousness to see how she was able to embrace all of Earth within her body. I realized that whales are not restricted by linear reality. Their brains are formulated to perceive the world from a much more holistic perspective, a perspective in which the boundaries of separate matter dissolve, a perspective that mystics, yogis, and shamans also share.

I recall the vision that Grace had in which Shiva was offering her the cosmic egg. What happens when we crack this egg open? What happens when we enter the quantum worlds where science and spirituality speak the same language, where the mystical and physical worlds are revealed to be the same? Will we follow the long spiral of eternity back to source? Or will we recognize that perhaps the egg never existed apart from the universe, and we were never separate from source to begin with!

The illusion of separate existence is the legacy of the Ancient Mind. We are conditioned to believe this is so, and therefore we experience our consciousness as being somehow trapped in matter. The morphogenetic field of our biological species responds to this shared belief by producing the limitations of matter that we are familiar with – aging, sickness, and death.

What if this could be changed? What if the unified field that Sri Aurobindo referred to as supramental consciousness could be brought down into the morphogenetic fields of the Earth in order to completely alter our relationship with matter? This, as I see it, was the work of Sri Aurobindo and the Mother. Quantum theory tells us that all matter is essentially one. If they could bring the supramental force down into their own bodies, it would equally impact upon the morphogenetic field of all matter on Earth.

They referred to unified matter as 'true matter', and felt that if they succeeded in bringing this supramental force down into their own bodies, changing their bodies into true matter, it would eventually work through the morphogenetic fields of humanity into all human bodies. A new supramental species would emerge. They did succeed in this effort, which is why they considered that the supramental force would most assuredly descend into human consciousness in years to come.

Bhagavan says that when mass enlightenment takes place, the Ancient Mind will become powerless. When this happens, our perceptions of reality will undergo a huge shift. We will no longer be bound by the laws of classical physics. We will begin to experience quantum reality in our physical bodies. Is this equivalent to Sri Aurobindo's descent of supramental consciousness?

I believe that Bhagavan's work is to take this force that is now established in the 'supramental fields' of the Earth, and to make it available to every person on Earth. It is significant to me that the Matrimandir, which the Mother designed as the focus through which the supramental force would descend on Earth, is shaped like a golden sphere. Is there a connection between this and the golden sphere that Bhagavan has programmed to descend into the crown chakra upon receiving the deeksha?

Sri Aurobindo said that a supramental species was to be born on Earth, which would be as different from humanity today as we are to the evolutions that have preceded us. Is this the process that will be initiated once the Ancient Mind is dissolved and the Golden Age is born? In Sri Aurobindo's epic poem, *Savitri*, he vividly describes this new race of humanity:

...I saw them cross the twilight of an age,
The sun-eyed children of a marvelous dawn,
Great creators with wide brows of calm,
The massive barrier-breakers of the world,
Laborers in the quarries of the gods...
The architects of immortality.
Into the fallen human sphere they came,
Faces that wore the Immortal's glory still...
Bodies made beautiful by the spirit's light...
Carrying the Dionysian cup of joy,
Lips chanting an unknown anthem of the soul,
Feet echoing in the corridors of Time.
High priests of wisdom, sweetness, might, and bliss;
Discoverers of beauty's sunlit ways...
Their tread one day shall change the suffering earth
And justify the light on Nature's face.
(Savitri, pp. 343–4)

Our collective experience of reality is shaped by the Ancient Mind. Because it is our shared reality we consider it to be the only possible reality. We cannot conceive of stepping outside this Ancient Mind to consider that other realities might exist. Until we are enlightened, we cannot begin to conceive that we can create any reality we choose to through the infinite creative power of the universe.

Many of you are probably familiar with 'The Matrix'. In this movie, Earth has been taken over by machines. Humans are cloned in breeding tanks and their central nervous systems tapped in order to provide the machines with the energy needed for their own functioning. In order to lull them into a false sense of purpose and security, however, an entire mass holographic reality has been created for the cloned humans where they appear to be eating, sleeping, working, watching TV, making love, and otherwise living normal lives.

This is the matrix, and it is policed by 'agents' that ensure that nobody comes to realize their true state of being. It is only when Neo, the archetypal hero, is 'unplugged' from the matrix, that he recognizes the extent of his captivity, and the madness of his former existence. With the help of his mentor, Morpheus, he slowly learns that he can create his own reality outside the matrix that is no longer subject to the rules of the matrix. In fact, the only limits are the limits of his own imagination. Once he discovers this, the agents have no more power over him, and he is free.

In a very real sense, the Ancient Mind is the Matrix. It creates an illusory sense of reality based on the shared assumptions of all those trapped within it. It is filled with fear, ugliness, and suffering. It is programmed to consider the body as separate. In its belief in separation, it utilizes the principle of entropy, which says that all energy winds down into chaos, ultimately leading to death. Nobody questions its existence. The Agents of social conditioning, ignorance, and self-doubt, ensure that nobody attempts to win their way to freedom. Yes, we might have all kinds of ideas and concepts about freedom, but all these are inside the Matrix as well.

Enlightenment is about unplugging from the Matrix! Once we recognize the extent to which we are programmed by the Ancient Mind, we cannot help but break free. When mass enlightenment happens, our collective sense of ego separation will dissolve. When this happens, we will be instantly freed from the conditioning and karma inherent within the Ancient Mind. Like Neo, we will discover as a species that we can break past our perceived limitations to create any reality we wish. It will be a dance of creation and freedom never before experienced. This, I believe, is what the Golden Age will be about.

As more and more of us get enlightened, we will step outside of time to dream new dreams, we will walk between the worlds with full awareness, we will birth new realities together, and we will allow the power of new creation to burst forth among us. We have experienced such a small portion of the physical universe, and even the physical universe is such a small aspect of the created universes. Can we imagine what it would be like to walk in the full power of divinity as limitless, multi-dimensional beings?

"Humanity is entering the most crucial phase of its existence," says Bhagavan. "The coming decade shall witness the most unprecedented and undreamt of changes in the course of its long evolution. There is nothing much humanity can do about it other than to understand the changes that are overpowering it. Towards the end, humanity will enter a new age – the Golden Age!"

Part 4

Conversation with Bhagavan

22. Conversation with Bhagavan

This is the transcript of a conversation I had with Bhagavan on October 8, 2004 in Golden City. It addresses issues of personal and global enlightenment through a process known as the "deeksha", which is an electrical transmission of divine energy resulting in neurobiological changes in the brain leading to states of enlightenment. It also covers questions about environmental catastrophes and earth changes, human death, and the advent of the long awaited Golden Age. It is also available as a CD and DVD.

~~~~
~~~~

Namaste Bhagavan, I am so grateful for your presence on this earth and in my life, and for the gift of enlightenment that you have given to me, and are giving to the world. For myself, I can say that there really seems like there is no individual self left, that who I am is simply the universe expressing through this body, experiencing itself moment to moment in a very fresh way. It seems like there is an emptiness here, an emptiness that is at the same time very full...

For the readers of my book and for people watching this video, I would first like to ask you to introduce yourself...

Well, I am known in India as Bhagavan. I am an avatar, an avatar who is specifically concerned about enlightening people and of course, also fulfilling their desires. I have been around for the past nearly 12 years or so. We have millions of followers, and a few thousand now who are enlightened. We can say that there is some kind of spiritual renaissance going on in the country here. We have been able to address all sections of society, men and women, young and old, rich and poor. There is now a tremendous seeking after enlightenment, a great passion now among large numbers of people to become enlightened, and so I have come to be considered as an avatar for enlightenment.

Bhagavan, for those may not be familiar with the term avatar, how would you define it?

In India, we have this concept of the avatar. An avatar could be a musical avatar, a mathematical avatar, a political avatar, or a spiritual avatar. An avatar is someone who comes with a specific mission on the planet and who is divinely inspired, and through whom divine energies flow. Avatars can come in every field of human activity. Many seem to think it is can only pertain to spiritual work, but it isn't so. But I happen to be a spiritual avatar.

You and Amma, your wife, are both avatars?

Yes we are both avatars, like two sides of the same coin. We have excellent understanding and communication, and sometimes we don't even have to talk to know what's going on. We work like one being when it comes to enlightenment and helping people.

Bhagavan, there have been so many avatars in human history, who have come and given different teachings, and helped to maybe enlighten a few people. What makes you so different?

Well, I think it is not about my being different. I think I have come at a different time. The other avatars prepared people for enlightenment, for liberation, but could not give it to them, not because they were not capable of giving it, but because the times were not ready for that. So I come at a time when earth's energies have changed, and man is very receptive, and it is possible to give him enlightenment. So my advantage is that I have come at the right time, a time when it is possible to give it to man.

Does this have something to do with our movement into the Golden Age?

It definitely has to do with the emergence of the Golden Age. In India it is believed that the Kali Yuga started sometime around 3002 BC and is supposed to have ended in 2002 AD.

By 2003 we are right into the Golden Age. That's why we began giving enlightenment publicly in the year 2003.

So it's only been one year.

It's only been one year.

How do you give enlightenment? How is it possible to give enlightenment?

Ah yes. Basically it is through the process of what is called 'deeksha', an electrical energy which transfers through some kind of a hole in the mind of man. We believe that the mind of man is like a wall, which divides man from God. The deeksha is an electrical energy which makes a hole in this wall, which we call the mind. Once that happens, then God and man can come to relate with each other. The way they relate has to do with his background, his conditioning, his aspirations, his education, so many factors. But it is God who gives enlightenment, whether you call it God or cosmic consciousness or nature, call it what you want... So that takes over and enlightenment is delivered through God. He is the one who delivers. Our job is to give the deeksha and make a hole in the mind, and then God does the rest. It's a very complex process that only God can do.

Is this something you have been preparing for for a very long time?

Yes, my whole life has been a preparation for this. Ever since I was a child, my only concern was how to liberate man from his suffering. These were not things that I arrived at through my own life experience, because I myself was a child, but rather I was forced to become concerned about man's suffering and to work for that. That is why I am an avatar, because I never arrived at these conclusions, I was just led into these things by a higher energy, a higher force, what you call the divine energy, or God.

Ever since I was a child I was made to do certain practices, which I did for many years. So that has given me the ability. So mostly I don't give deekshas. I let others give deeksha. I am more like a powerhouse, and the others are like step down transformers who can receive this energy and pass it on to people. So my function is to remain as a powerhouse for some time. So this is how deeksha is given and how enlightenment or God realization occurs.

So when you give deeksha you speak of this deeksha as a neurobiological process that affects the brain?

Yes, when we give deeksha it is like the passing on of an electrical energy that affects the brain, the spinal cord, and what we call the ductless glands or the 'chakras'. So most of the work is being done on the frontal lobes and the parietal lobes of the brain. There is an activation of the frontal lobes, and a deactivation of the parietal lobes, plus some energies are sent into the ductless glands to reactivate these chakras. So all this in turn produces a hole in the mind, and a link is established between God and man. Thereafter what happens is God's work. Up to then, of course, we can do certain things.

Right. So when you speak about losing the 'self', that's what happens when you make this hole in the wall.

When you make the hole in the wall, then God can take over, and then he works on the senses, liberating the senses from the mind, from the clutches of the mind. When that happens you lose your 'self'. That part of the work happens through God himself. As He is the creator, he works like a computer to rearrange the brain, and He takes over.

So each person's enlightenment is absolutely unique then.

It's absolutely unique. It depends on his background, his conditioning, what happened in his childhood, his own seeking, his religious conditioning. So all these things are involved.

Bhagavan, many many people have been seeking for many many lifetimes, and been through all kinds of practices and sadhanas and rituals and ceremonies and traditions and many times they feel they have only been able to go so far, and none have been able to actually cross over into enlightenment. So how is this different?

When I look at a person, I don't see him as a first-timer. I only see millions of years behind him. I believe that all of humanity has finished all the work they need to do. I think everybody has been well prepared through so many lives. And therefore now is the time to get it. All the hard work has been done. I believe everybody has done the hard work, and now the fruit is there to be had.

Yes, it must be such a relief for many people to hear that.

Yes, that's why I see everyone as a seeker, everybody has done their sadhana, everybody is ready. I cannot say so and so is not ready.

So there's no one who is not a seeker?

There is no one who is not a seeker. They could be seeking in different ways...

They could be seeking without even knowing they are seeking.

Without knowing they are seeking...

So as this work progresses, is it possible that more and more people will become enlightened who have no idea about enlightenment, who have never been seeking enlightenment, it will simply just happen?

Yes, what is likely to happen is that there are now people who are enlightened who are able to give deekshas to people who are able to get into good states. But very soon, maybe a few months from now, those who will receive deeksha from them will naturally become enlightened. And not only that, they will be able to give deeksha to others and make them enlightened. This process will continue for some time. There will come a time when without deeksha the whole of mankind is going to make it. Once the critical level is reached there is going to be a spontaneous occurrence across the planet.

What will this look like in practical terms?

In practical terms the world will look very different. We will not be able to talk about me being an Indian or you being an American or somebody else being an African. we cannot talk in terms of races and nationalities, or I can't say I'm a Hindu, I'm a Christian, I'm a Muslim.

So all these things which divide man will just disappear. All these things will just drop off. There will be no need for these things. All these divisions will not exist. We will become just human beings. We will become one family. It's not a concept, this will just happen. This is when we will truly become humans. But as long as we are going to define ourselves in terms of nationalities, religions, cultures, race, we will still continue to be tribal and very primitive. We are becoming human now. It will definitely happen.

What about people who are still into power, control, and ego games, and who may not want to get enlightened?

Yes, people who stubbornly resist enlightenment will also naturally become enlightened. At that point there won't be any resisting it. Nobody can say "I will stay out of enlightenment". That is not possible. It's a natural occurrence. It's human evolution. So all these power games and ego games will just stop. You can just not do it anymore. The brain will function differently.

That's amazing. So even the people who are consciously and adamantly refusing to even think about sharing the earth with other people, who are trying to control the resources of the earth and creating environmental devastation for their own benefit, whether companies, governments, businesses, or individuals, this will all change?

Yes, all this will dramatically change. Man will soon realize that the earth is a living organism, he depends on it like his Mother, so no one will even think of harming the earth. This won't take some kind of education; it will be a natural happening. This is what will happen. So we are going to see a very different earth, a very different world. I am not speculating. I am just speaking very directly from the visions thousands of people have had in the last decade from various continents.

Bhagavan there are many scientists who predict, based on what is happening on the planet today – global warming, possible ice age coming, the quality of air and water, and so on – that there could be a major environmental catastrophe, and that we might even end up wiping out all life on the planet. How can you be so sure that there will be a planetary enlightenment?

The predictions are quite true, but what they are not aware of is that, as we have seen in our visions, a great transformation is sweeping across the planet which will in turn prevent these things from happening. Already we are seeing signs of people becoming enlightened, and how it affects the environment. We are able to see this on a very small scale. And from that we are able to predict that on a global scale this transformation is going to occur. This is what is going to save the earth. If that does not happen, then what the scientists are predicting could very well come true.

So an example could be that if a village gets enlightened, and there has been a drought for the past few years, then the monsoons...

The monsoons will come, yes. It is happening in many places in India. We are seeing it.

So similarly when there are predictions of major earthquakes, volcanic activity, pole shifts even, then as people become enlightened, this will alter our relationship with the earth...

We could save the earth. That is why we are telling people "the house is on fire, let us move faster, let us hurry up".

Yes, this is a very important message for people to hear. There are so many people in despair and hopelessness, so many good people who have given up any kind of future for the earth because of what they see with their outer eyes.

Yes, but there is no need for them to lose hope. Because things are going to change dramatically. In a very unexpected way things are going to change.

Yes, I am so happy to hear that. As people become enlightened, and as the planet becomes enlightened as a collective, how will that change the physical quality of the earth?

There is a very close correlation between human consciousness and the physical process occurring on the planet. So the moment that conflict levels are reduced in human consciousness, you will find dramatic changes at the earth level also. So you will find a reduction of insects and pests in the crops, and nature behaving in a much better way without the need for chemicals. All these things are a natural consequence of the reduction of conflict in human consciousness. There is such a close correlation between the two. This also we are seeing on a small scale at the village level.

So as humans become enlightened, then our relationship with the environment will change, species that have become extinct will come back, the oceans will become depolluted, and so on.

Yes, we have seen remarkable things happening on a small scale, so we believe it can happen on a large scale also. So that's why we are so confident that these things will happen. Otherwise there seems to be no hope in living at all.

Yes, otherwise there doesn't seem to be any point in going on. Bhagavan, one question I have is about yours and Amma's consciousness which pervades the deeksha. How is it possible with so many people receiving the deeksha now that you are able to track what's happening with everybody individually?

We actually function on two levels. When I am having this conversation with you, certain things are switched off so that I can hold this meaningful conversation. But at other times the switches are on and we can experience a lot of human beings at once and what is going on in their minds and their consciousness, and we can interfere and do many things. That dimension is not known to man. I am not claiming this as something special to me, because whatever I am experiencing I believe in making others also experience, and there are also others now at that level who can similarly experience a few hundred beings at the same time. This is a faculty that is very natural to man and will start to open up in many people. To me it happens very naturally. Because of what happened to me in my early life I can focus on a 100,000-strong crowd and go into them and do many things.

So you are able to go into the collective consciousness...

Yes, it happens very easily and very naturally. And others too are now able to do it to some extent. Soon it will start happening in a bigger way.

And that's very much a part of enlightenment.

That's very much a part of enlightenment, in fact many things will start happening after enlightenment. We are not talking very much about it because it is going to happen very naturally. Enlightenment is not going to stop at just being aware of things, or just being joyful or being in bliss. There is a lot more to it. But these will follow in the months coming.

One question which may sound a little strange, how is your consciousness as an avatar different from the consciousness of someone who gets enlightened?

At this point in time the only difference could be in the intensity of the awareness or the intensity of the bliss, but otherwise there is no basic fundamental difference. But as these nadis open up and become stronger, his awareness levels will also increase and the gap will soon close. But it may take a little time. But fundamentally there is no difference. Except I do have some additional facilities. Like I can see what is going on in some other place, what's happening in somebody's mind, how I can help them. I can really interfere in helping their life by taking up a strong sankalpa, a strong wish. These too people will be able to acquire in the course of time. Already a few of them have acquired this in small measure.

So as people deepen into their enlightenment, these will be things that anyone is capable of?

Yes, as your concern for people grows, these things naturally start happening. It's all a matter of how concerned you are about others. As you go deeper and deeper into enlightenment your concern also increases. Along with this, these things also start happening.

Yes, seems as if an entirely new species is arising.

Yes, it's more like that, an entirely new species is emerging.

Bhagavan, there are so many different religions in the world today. What is your attitude towards all the different faiths?

I believe that different religions are required to handle the different needs of people. I have seen people sometimes require a particular religion to handle a particular problem, or their background needs the input of a particular religion. I personally have never had any difficulty with people of any faith. Because the deeksha is a neutral thing and the deeksha only activates a certain area of the brain or deactivates it, and the person only discovers what his religion taught him. So he discovers the truths of his own faith. What I do or teach is not a new faith or religion, it is not anything new at all, it merely helps you to discover what you have been seeking all these years. So I personally have no conflict with the people of any faith.

So once people are enlightened, the Muslim will experience his unity with Allah, the Christian will experience himself a Christ, a Buddhist will experience Buddha consciousness, and so on?

And so on. There is absolutely no conflict at all. That's why I am saying that soon there will be no divisions of man, saying I belong to this religion or that religion, you know, we are going to become one family. This is going to be a reality.

There is this beautiful song by John Lennon where he speaks of that.

Yes, and we are seeing this happening, especially in the areas where we are working, we are seeing it happening.

Yes, it seems that the differences between religions have only to do with ego, nothing to do with the essence of that religion.

Yes.

Bhagavan, you speak of different stages, different aspects of enlightenment. You speak of the flowering of the heart, you speak of the witness consciousness, you speak about oneness. Could you describe this in more detail?

Yes, the first thing that often happens in the process of enlightenment is the flowering of the heart. You for the first time discover real compassion, real love for human beings. But as this becomes deeper you lose a sense of separateness. Even at this point we really do not call you fully enlightened. We call you fully enlightened only when you are experiencing reality as it is. To experience reality as it is these are some kinds of pre-requisites. Very rarely it happens suddenly in a big way. So these may be called stages of enlightenment. Enlightenment itself is experiencing reality as it is.

Is that equivalent to oneness?

It is equivalent to oneness. But of course, oneness itself just takes off from there and finally becomes oneness with God, or oneness with cosmic consciousness. It is the ultimate oneness. But that could be difficult for some people, to say that man and God could become one. That some people may not accept, but it is a reality that people can become one with God.

You speak of designing your own God. What do you mean by that?

When I speak of designing your own God I do not mean that you create your own God. God is someone who creates you, and you do not create God. But the way he is going to treat you and the way he is going to conduct himself with you depends on how you expect him to conduct himself with you. This is taken from the Hindu concept of 'bhakta paradeena', that God is dependent on the devotee. So if you want him to be a friend he behaves like a friend. If you want him to behave like a mother, he behaves like a mother. So it is in your hands to design the way he is going to behave with you. That's how I say you design your own God.

So certain aspects, certain views of God will make it easier to actually receive this gift.

Yes, it can be very easy to receive this gift. If your concept of God is a very friendly one then you don't even have to pray. You just ask it and he gives it to you. Thousands of people have this kind of relationship. I am only talking about when people have actually achieved it, not before that. So people have made God their friend, a very friendly God. This includes, Christians, Muslims, Hindus, people of all faiths.

And God is masculine as well as feminine?

God is masculine as well as feminine, or light or formless. Many have only a formless God. Many have it as just light. Some even have him as both male and female. Each person has complete freedom. It's the individual's choice.

You also speak of designing your own enlightenment.

Your own enlightenment, yes, like for example, you can design how much of heart you want, or how much of oneness you want, or how much of experiencing your reality you want. Again it depends on your passion, the kind of books you have read, the kind of seeking you have had.

So it's really the beginning of a lifelong journey or exploration...

Exploration, yes. And you can change it also, in the course of time, you can change it. In practice we find that people achieve different states of enlightenment.

What determines what state of enlightenment a person receives? Does it have to do with karmic factors or does it have to do with your belief systems?

It has a lot to do with your belief systems, closely followed by your karma. Very often it has to do with your belief systems, the kind of conditioning you have gone through. But you can change it if you want to at some point in time, if you feel like it. So that's why I am saying you can design your God, and you can design your enlightenment.

Bhagavan, I remember when I was young I was very fascinated by the life and teachings of Jesus, and always wondered what it would be like to be born in his times, to be one of his disciples, when he sent them out to go heal the sick and relieve suffering. What is fascinating to me now is that the same kinds of miracles, the same kinds of healings are beginning to happening now with the deekshas and with other circumstances. Would you like to say something about that?

Yes, this is the continuation of that work that Christ left behind. This should have happened in fact 2000 years ago, this transformation of man, but for some reason it got aborted. But now the same thing has come back. So in the deekshas people are getting in touch with Christ consciousness, especially in the west. They are discovering the same consciousness which Christ was trying to give them. It is no different from that. In fact I would say that would be true Christianity, as Christ intended it to be.

Yes, Christ said "I and the Father are One".

Yes.

So from that consciousness, miracles are possible. So as people experience the same consciousness today the same miracles are being evident.

Yes, exactly.

You mention that here are certain miracles taking place in Orissa.

Yes there is a place in Orissa, called Gutagaon, where thousands of people come, and get healed. There is another place called Bhimavaram where surgeries are done on them as they come and lie down in front of the srimurti.

Like miracle surgeries. Like psychic surgeries?

Miracle surgeries, yes. More and more this will be happening around the country and around the world. These are not miracles that I go and do,. they are spontaneous miracles occurring around the planet. I personally do not do any miracles like that. I am not a miracle worker in that sense.

But you train people to become miracle workers.

Yes, around them these miracles happen.

So it's really cosmic consciousness that allows the miracles to take place. So the fact that is happening more and more, and that enlightenment is happening more and more, you have spoken about this in relationship to what you have called the 'morphogenetic fields'. Could you describe that phenomenon?

Yes, for example this phenomenon is about 12 years old, and we have found that at certain intervals it becomes more powerful. So what we have discovered is that the more people get that state it becomes easier for other people get that state, whether it is in connection with healings or the enlightened state or other states of consciousness. We find that people who come later are getting it more easily and much faster. So obviously there is a field which is absorbing all this transformation and able to transfer it to others much faster. That's how the morphogenetic fields are really helping. We can see it in action.

There is a psychologist in America, David Hawkins. And he has devised a scale of consciousness from 0 to 1000. At the bottom end of the scale are emotions like guilt, shame, fear, whereas on the upper end you have love and joy and enlightenment. What he says is that one person who is holding the state of joy or love or enlightenment can actually counterbalance thousands or even millions of people who are holding the states of guilt, shame and fear that so many people are stuck in. So what he says is that this is also a morphogenetic field and what is taking place is that because it doesn't take a large number of people, as long as they are high on the consciousness scale, they can actually create a huge wave of enlightenment.

Yes that's very true. That is the purpose of the sages and saints; they have to counterbalance the other negative energies. That is why we believe that once we have 64,000 people, that will be enough for transforming the whole of mankind.

Why 64,000?

Somehow that seems to be the necessary number for making this happen very spontaneously... These are factors which have been revealed to us. We don't fully understand the dynamics, but these were revealed to us. We go on the basis of revelation. It is not just something that comes to one person, but if it is something that happens to many people over a long period of time, that is what we accept as revelation. That becomes our road map.

How long will it take to get 64,000 people enlightened?

It could take anywhere from one year to 6 years. It can happen very fast also. It depends on how quickly people respond. It could happen in a few months time also. So we can't really specify the time here. It can happen very fast, or it can take a little more time.

So now you are training people to give deekshas themselves, and this will be a part of this. They will move out across the earth and they will begin to give deekshas and make people enlightened, and then eventually, like you said, it will happen through a touch, a glance, a prayer...

It could happen very very fast. Let's say people read your book that could be some kind of deeksha. Or they can flock to your talks or programs where you are giving deeksha, and it could happen very very fast. It can happen very fast really. People must be very serious. That's all that is required.

I know some musicians who have gone through the deeksha training, and so as they perform the music, then that itself could be a deeksha.

Yes. And one thing likely to happen, as people read your book, they could also get some kind of deeksha. That's also very much possible.

I notice that when I was writing the book it was flowing through in such an amazing fashion, the entire book was written in 10 days. In fact, I felt your presence coming through so strongly. So I am sure it is a deeksha.

Yes, it is more like our architect who designed our Oneness Temple. It just flowed through him, and in no time at all it was ready. It was just lying before him.

You said about the Oneness Temple, that when people go in to worship, people can come in from any religious faith, but what they will see is a reflection of their own God.

Yes, it is a very strange temple, and there will be a strange throne there, an empty throne. And when people from any faith will come and worship they will see their God or a sign of their God's presence on the throne. It will only be visible to them. They can pray in any fashion they want. And they will see their God on the throne. That's what is so unique about it.

So it is an inner revelation. It also reminds me of the phenomenon that is growing known as the 'phala deeksha'. What actually happens?

In phala deeksha the God whom they worship appears before them. They could have a dialogue with that God and ask them for whatever they want or any clarifications they need about their life. It is a great dialogue between man and God. And God may grant them their wish, and in case he is not granting it he will give them a reason why he is not granting it. So it is a one to one relationship between man and God. So he gets what he wants.

So it is no longer dependent on faith. It is a real life experience.

It is a real life experience. It does not depend on your faith.

It shows the change in the relationship between man and God.

Yes. There is a change. Something very epochal is happening here. There is a definite change. God is coming very close to man. And man too. It is a lost relationship. They were supposed to be very close in the last Golden Age. They are supposed to have walked and talked together, you know. Then there was a strange alienation between man and God. And it generated in subsequent yugas. So now that the Golden Age is back, man and God have to come together. They become friends again. That's it.

I see the veils are beginning to thin between the dimensions and lokas. One question that it brings up for me is the idea of death, because so many people are afraid to die, especially when they are conditioned by beliefs about hell, if they have done something bad, or even believe that they have done something bad, that they will go to hell. What actually happens to people as they make that passage?

What happens is that as people die and they are very scared of hell or of being judged by God, then very often they do not continue their journey. They get stuck in the earth sphere as earthbound spirits. That is an unfortunate thing that is happening. If people of different faiths do the necessary rituals and ceremonies then it is definitely possible to help them. But more important would be to make them talk to God and realize that God is very friendly and is not going to stand in judgment over them. But this is going to require a shift in man's thinking. I think that's the best way to liberate man. He has to get friendly with his God, otherwise there is needless trouble.

So the actual passage of death is very beautiful and peaceful?

It's very very beautiful. The process of dying is a very beautiful process. But for most people, it takes about three days to realize they are dead. Somehow it takes that much time. That's why people have to go through ceremonies to help them realize they are dead and then to prepare them for their journey to meet God. So if that can take place it is very easy. But if on the other hand fear is put into the person they will hang around. Then they will have to be helped.

So there are spirit helpers who can assist them to go to the appropriate lokas?

Yes, that's why when people come to us we work with them to help their ancestors, their parents and grandparents to be cleared. And once these people move away from the earth sphere the person can actually feel the liberation, they will feel a lightness. It's not something to be believed in, but it can be experienced.

Bhagavan, what about people who have died? When global enlightenment happens, will they also be...

They will be spontaneously enlightened. It's not only for the living but also for the dead.

So then they can choose to reincarnate again on this earth or somewhere else?

It's up to them whether they want reincarnate on the earth sphere, or some other sphere, or some other planet. It's all up to them. Such is the freedom given to man.

Bhagavan, there are many people who have been longing their whole life for love, who feel like this has eluded them, who are so afraid to love, who are so afraid to receive love, what would you say to people like that?

Yes, I think they will soon be soaked and bathed in love. I think there will soon be spontaneous occurrences of this. Before enlightenment occurs people will have discovered love, I think. And that will soon be followed by enlightenment itself. And that will be followed by oneness with God. I think that will be the order.

So enlightenment, God-realization, love...

Enlightenment, God-realization, love all these things are going to happen, people won't have to try and get there, these will just spontaneously happen.

I think that's the biggest gift that you are offering, that there is no striving necessary, in fact the striving itself can be a block, an obstacle to receiving it, because then the mind feels like it can do something.

Like it can do something, yes. The poor mind cannot do anything, it is conflict ridden, it is in opposition with itself, it is repetitive in nature, it is too ancient. So really it can't do much. It has to realize it is helpless and give up. That's when grace can take over.

You speak about the mind as the ancient mind. What do you imply by that?

By that I imply that basically its structure has not changed. That fear is at the core of the human mind. Earlier it could have been the fear of a tiger or lion; today it is the fear of the stock market or the fear of losing your job. Then you were very anxious abut the weather, now you are anxious about your job or other things. The same craving is there, the same desires are there. The objects of desire have changed but the desire to be something else is still there. You see, fundamentally man has not changed, that's why I call the mind very ancient. Only the objects have changed, the objects of craving, the objects of fear, the objects of anxiety, they have changed.

But fundamentally it is the same old mind, living continuously in fear, living continuously in becoming, moving from where you are to where you want to be. It does not stay put. It is not where it should be. It mainly lives in fear. And basically there is no change in man. So I do not see any difference between Homo sapiens and Neanderthal man. We have had limited experience of people who have lived earlier, and we see that fundamentally they are the same.

So when we are enlightened we can leave this mind behind.

You can leave this mind behind, yes. You can become completely free of the mind. I am talking of a transformation where you become free of the mind. I am not focusing so much on a transformation within the mind. That the psychologists and the philosophers can do. And they are doing a fairly good job. So I don't have to waste time on that. But I am talking of becoming free of the mind itself.

Bhagavan, do you have any plans to travel around the world?

Certainly not in the near future. Maybe sometime, it's very possible. I don't really need to travel. I can do my work from wherever I am.

Do you feel that at some point your work will be over?

Most certainly, yes. The moment the world is enlightened, my work is over. The moment humanity becomes one humanity, one complete humanity, and all the divisions have ceased, my work is over. I am here to remove all divisions in whatever form they might exist.

So Bhagavan would you like to say any final words to readers of this book, or to people watching this video?

I would like to tell them that though humanity faces a lot of obstacles, and danger seems to be lurking around the corner, I would like to tell them that redemption is around the corner, that we are going to make it!

Bhagavan, I am so grateful to be in your presence, and to know that this redemption is around the corner. I am sure many many people around the world echo my sentiments, just to know that there is hope and that there is a plan, that we are entering into a Golden Age, and that the deeksha is possible now, that it can actually transform people's lives so completely and so beautifully in a way that was never possible before. So please accept my heartfelt gratitude.

It has been so nice talking to you.

Thank you. Namaste.

Appendix I

Doorway to Eternity

The question I had always asked myself was, are we birthing a Golden Age, or are we spiraling into extinction? It would be no exaggeration to state that if we look only at the outer physical realities, we are in extreme global crisis. Where does hope lie for our planet?

As I researched my previous book, "Doorway to Eternity: A Guide to Planetary Ascension", I had come to some understandings and conclusions about the coming mass enlightenment of humanity, what is often known in the New Age movement as the Shift of the Ages. These conclusions are very similar to what Bhagavan has said about the mass enlightenment of humanity by 2012. I would like to summarize some of this research, spanning various ancient calendar systems, mystic prophecies and visions, as well as some very interesting cosmological and geological findings in recent years.

I will begin with the Mayan calendar, which in recent times has become quite well known as a prophetic guide for humanity's evolutionary journey. There have been many interpretations of this calendar system through the years, not all of which agree with each other. One of these comes through a Swedish researcher, Carl Johan Calleman, author of 'Enlightenment: The Mayan Calendar as our Guide to the Future' (www.calleman.com). Grace and I had the privilege of meeting Calleman when he was here in Golden City for the Experience Festival, and developed a close friendship with this wonderful, wise, warm human being. He has the razor sharp focused mind of a brilliant scientist, and the playfulness and sweetness of a young child.

Calleman provides an interpretation of this calendar that is especially fascinating to me because it allows us to see the energies of creation at work in linear history. It is not my intention here to explain this in any great detail, except to say that the Mayan understanding of cosmic cycles allowed them to pinpoint future events with a great deal of accuracy. Calleman applies this understanding to these current times, and recognizes Bhagavan as one whose mission is to bring these cycles into fulfillment. He has also personally met Bhagavan and exchanged ideas with him.

According to Calleman, we have just begun the 8th out of 9 cycles of creation, all of which simultaneously end in 2012. Each time we move into a successive creation cycle, evolution speeds up, and a greater dispensation of avataric energies becomes available. There is a cosmic order to these creation cycles. Each creation cycle goes through a succession of predictable shifts in energy as it moves towards completion, just as a seed moves through predictable stages as it grows into a tree.

It would take too much space to correlate these cycles with current events in history, but it is fascinating to see how Bhagavan's mission has been following the same patterns of ebb and flow. The Mayans believed that the year 2012 would signify the end of linear time, and represent a time of great cosmic shift.

Bhagavan's vision fits this timetable perfectly. An avatar descends to Earth in response to human need, and in fulfillment of cosmic plan. I see the synchronicity between the ending of the Mayan calendar and Bhagavan's mission for Planetary Enlightenment as the realization of a vast divine destiny, a destiny that even goes far beyond Earth herself.

There is some very interesting research going on by a group of scientists at the Russian National Academy of Sciences in Siberia, headed by Dr. Alexei Dmetriev. Our Sun is surrounded by a magnetic field known as the heliosphere. The glowing plasma at the leading edge of this heliosphere, they say, has increased in luminosity by 1000 percent in the past few years, from 10 Astronomical units to 100 Astronomical Units! The conclusion they derive is that we are moving into a region of space where the energy is more highly charged.

This highly charged energy is exciting the plasma, which is affecting the radiations within the Sun, which in turn is affecting all the planets in our solar system. They predict this is all working up to a crescendo where there will be a sudden expansion in the basic harmonic wavelength emitted by the Sun, which in turn will cause a sudden shift in the consciousness of all life in the solar system!

During my experience of cosmic consciousness, I literally experienced Bhagavan as being the physical embodiment of the Sun here on Earth. As he brings this cycle to a close in response to a cosmic timetable, I can see the relationship between his presence on Earth and the expansion of the heliosphere!

Some people refer to this highly charged region of space as the 'photon belt', others the 'galactic superwave', others yet the 'manasic ring'. It is a region of expanded galactic frequencies that many believe will propel us into a higher order of evolution. Perhaps all this is synchronistically aligned with Bhagavan's avataric consciousness, preparing for the incredible shift to come as we enter the Golden Age.

As Bhagavan's work continues to expand, I expect there will be even bigger changes in the heliosphere. Another phenomenon occurring today is the increase in sunspot activity. There are well known cycles of sunspot activity that scientists have been charting for several decades, but what has been taking place in the past few years has been throwing them into a quandary. If this phenomenally increasing sunspot activity is related to Bhagavan's presence on Earth, I can only expect that this will continue to increase over the next few years as well, and also closely align with the periodicity of the Mayan creation cycles.

The 9th creation cycle begins in February 2011, and ends, synchronistically with all the other creation cycles, with the end-point of the Mayan calendar. This signifies another major acceleration in cosmic evolution, culminating in a massive quantum leap. It is also the time when astronomers tell us that we will be crossing the galactic equator.

The galactic equator is the central plane of our Milky Way galaxy. We cross this equator every 13,000 years or so. Every time we have crossed the galactic equator in the past, geologists tell us, this has been accompanied by major cataclysmic activity. The last time this happened coincided with the sinking of an entire continent on Earth, what is referred to in our legends as the sinking of Atlantis.

Geologist Gregg Braden associates this periodicity with the reversal of Earth's magnetic poles, while Douglas Vogt and Gary Sultan also associate this with a nova effect of the sun, in which a blaze of super-ionized plasma would be pulsed out throughout the solar system. All this could have a potentially disastrous effect on the Earth.

Astrophysicist Paul LaViolette speaks of a 'galactic superwave', a pulse that emanates periodically from the center of our Milky Wave galaxy. It expands spherically across the galaxy. According to him, our solar system is getting ready to experience the next pulse of this superwave. Perhaps this is equivalent to the phenomenon I referred to earlier as the 'photon belt', in response to which the Russian scientists were noticing the dramatic increase in intensity of our heliosphere.

In any case, he too speaks of what could happen as the superwave interacts with our Sun. He says that as the galactic superwave expands simultaneously out through the galaxy, it creates a null point in which magnetic and gravitational fields collapse. As our Sun experiences this collapse, it would release gas shells around the Sun, resulting in a massive ejection of its corona throughout our solar system. This sudden expansion followed by a contraction, according to LaViolette, could cause some rather major cataclysmic activity on Earth.

Is this why Bhagavan is so insistent that mankind must be enlightened by 2012? When the nova of the sun happens it could potentially cause the extinction of life on Earth. It could also potentially propel humanity into a huge evolutionary leap forward. It all depends on our state of consciousness and the subsequent dimensional space that we occupy. An enlightened humanity could use this opportunity to ride the solar wave into the experience of what some have called 'planetary ascension', a totally unprecedented event.

Geologist Gregg Braden examines the Earth's geological records to indicate that we are getting close to what he calls a 'zero point'. This zero point is the convergence of two trends that are currently taking place on Earth: a lowering of the intensity of her magnetic fields, and a rise in her base harmonic frequency as measured by what is known as the 'Schumann resonance'.

The magnetic field of the Earth has been gradually deteriorating over the past few centuries, and it is expected that at a certain point of time this deterioration will accelerate very suddenly, and cause a polar reversal. Does the completion of this 13,000 year cycle coincide with the quantum shift of consciousness expected in 2012? My sense is that the Ancient Mind that Bhagavan refers to is a subtle electromagnetic field that permeates the body of the Earth. As these fields collapse and re-orient themselves, so will the Ancient Mind. The three days that it takes to re-orient these fields could well be the three days that Bhagavan refers to when all humanity will suddenly become enlightened.

Braden says that the Schumann resonance of Earth, which has been vibrating at close to 8 hertz (cycles per second) for hundreds of years, has suddenly started to increase in frequency over the past few decades. He expects that when we reach 'zero point' – perhaps by 2012 – this will stabilize at approximately 13 cycles per second.

Research with brain waves and consciousness indicates that brainwaves of 8-13 cycles per second dominate the alpha state of consciousness, which is a dreaming state. The waking state is known as beta consciousness, and reveals brainwave patterns vibrating at 13-21 cycles per second. Isn't it interesting that human consciousness will soon be collectively stepping up from our current dreaming state into a waking state? It will literally be the moment of our awakening!

I have come to believe that our 13,000-year journey back and forth across the galactic equator also coincides with the Vedic cycle of the yugas. In astronomical terms it is related to what is called the 'precession of the equinoxes', which is a 26,000-year cycle which gives us the astrological ages we are familiar with. Although the classical understanding of the Yugas portrays these cycles as being millions of years long, Sri Yukteswar, a disciple of Babaji Mahavatar, introduced a new understanding of these yugas by correlating them with the precession of the equinoxes.

If my understanding of this is accurate, it means that every time we cross the galactic equator we move from a Kali Yuga into a Satya Yuga. It is an instantaneous transition. It is like water turning into steam. At a particular temperature, as water continues being heated, there is what is known as a 'phase transition', and it suddenly changes state. This phenomenon can be seen throughout nature, and can even be noted in the journey of evolution, as indicated in the parable of the 'hundredth monkey'. Some refer to it as a quantum leap.

All of these findings derive from careful research by various scientists. Since I have provided extensive references and far more detail in my book, *Doorway to Eternity: A Guide to Planetary Ascension*, I will not go into great detail at this point. My research had led me to deeply appreciate the pivotal nature of these times, and I felt in my heart of hearts that we would somehow 'make it', but it was only when I met Bhagavan that I was given the final confirmation and understood how.

"By their fruits ye shall know them", said Jesus. It is easy for anybody to make claims about anything. It is only when you see the claims being fulfilled that you can choose to trust or to believe.

This has been so for me. I have not only experienced my own enlightenment, but through my research into cosmic cycles, was convinced of the necessity for such a mass enlightenment in precisely the same sequence that Bhagavan says it will happen. Experiencing his 'sankalpa' through my own direct experience of cosmic consciousness was the final proof I needed. Bhagavan says this mass enlightenment will affect not only those who alive in their physical bodies at the time, but also all those who have died and inhabiting other dimensions or 'lokas'.

Interestingly, Bhagavan's birthday falls on 13 Ahau, which is the last signature of the Mayan galactic calendar, or 'Tzolkin'. Calleman says that 13 Ahau is the energy at which there are no filters blocking the passage of cosmic light. As all the nine creation cycles move towards this tzolkin energy, all human beings will come into resonance with this enlightening energy. If Bhagavan's plan succeeds, this is when we will move into collective Enlightenment!

Just as individual enlightenment is both an event and a process, so is collective enlightenment, and our transition into the Golden Age. It is like being born, says Bhagavan. By the time we enter the Golden Age in 2012, a lot of things will have changed on the planet. There will be no more poverty, there will be health and abundance for all, there will be new forms of education, government, science and medicine. There will be alternative energy sources, new forms of fuel, and technologies that are earth-friendly. There will be more love within the family, including the extended family of nations. This is how you will know that the Golden Age has been born.

Even so, this will only be the beginning. It will not yet be a perfect society. Once the child is born, it still has to grow up. The Golden Age will last a thousand years, and there will be lots of room for growth and improvement. There will even be far-reaching genetic changes within the human species. The new human will be androgynous, more translucent, and capable of using far more of his brain potential. We will consciously travel in and out of our bodies at will. Reproduction will take place differently than it does today, through a process of co-creative manifestation of intent. And as a species, we will move collectively into deeper and deeper states of divine oneness!

The Christian *Book of Revelations* says that when the seventh angel blows his trumpet, "time will be no more".

The Mayans, in their calendar system echo this understanding, and give us a timetable for this event, which is the same timetable that Bhagavan is working with. What does this statement mean? I believe they are referring to linear time, which has to do with the nature of reality inherent in the duality of Ancient Mind. As an enlightened planet, we will move into what we could call 'cosmic time', which will be an entirely different experience.

As more and more of us get enlightened, we will step outside of time to dream new dreams, we will walk between the worlds with full awareness, we will birth new realities together, and we will allow the power of new creation to burst forth among us. We have experienced such a small portion of the physical universe, and even the physical universe is such a small aspect of the created universes. Can we imagine what it would be like to walk in the full power of divinity as limitless, multi-dimensional beings?

Appendix 2

Enlightenment and the Brain

A Scientific Commentary of the Teachings of Sri Kalki

By Christian Opitz
(christian@powerorganics.com)

The state of enlightenment has been associated with a change of brain function in various spiritual traditions. Sri Kalki, the founder of the Golden Age Foundation has now expanded this traditional knowledge about the role of the brain in spiritual transformation. The deeksha or energy transmission that lies at the heart of the practical side of his teaching is designed to bring about a permanent change in actual neurological patterns. His statements about the changes induced in the brain through deeksha can be confirmed with the most advanced findings in physics and neuroscience. In the following, I would like to present a comparison between some of Sri Kalki's statements and my own findings in studying the brain through the means of physics and neurophysiology:

1. **Sri Kalki describes a disconnection of activity in the parietal lobes as an essential event in the enlightenment process.**

The parietal lobes host what some neuroscientists call the Orientation Association Area or OAA. The function of the OAA is to give us orientation is space. You may take it for granted that you can tie your shoelaces and walk through a door, but this is only possible due to furious neurological activity in the rear part of the parietal lobes. Brain damage to this area makes the smallest tasks like grabbing a glass of water impossible, because the injured brain cannot perceive a distinction between the hand, the glass and the space in between.

On the physical level, the ability to perceive boundaries and distinction is essential for our ability to carry out tasks. However in the human brain, the OAA is chronically overactive. This stimulates the amygdala – hippocampus connection, a pair of brain centers that is designed to give a sense of meaning to perceptions registered as important. If the OAA, which is designed to create a perception of distinction and separation to a useful degree, is hyperactive the amygdala – hippocampus connection has no choice but to interpret this hyperactivity by assuming that separation has more reality than just on the level of physical objects like your hand and a glass.

The conclusion is that we are fundamentally, existentially separate from anything else. The sense of self, which the brain creates constantly in reaction to perception of what is perceived at "other" than self (the basic premise of object – relations theory in developmental psychology) is then endowed with a sense of absolute, distinct separation of self from everything else. Neuroscience has shown that in deep meditation or prayer, the OAA in the parietal lobe is temporarily blocked from neurological input. This can give temporary states of vastly expanded consciousness, as the sense of separate self cannot find its usual boundaries and expands to find them. However, this is a temporary experience, dependent on altered brain function such as the suppression of neurological input to the OAA that a permanent abiding in oneness consciousness is almost impossible to attain in this way.

This echoes Sri Kalki's statement that enlightenment has to be given; it cannot be attained by self effort. The deekshas seem to induce a process of transformation in the parietal lobes that permanently changes their function to a natural level, where physical boundaries can be perceived but unnatural overactivity ceases. The amygdala – hippocampus would then have no more reason or stimulation to create the sense of an existentially separate self.

2. Sri Kalki says that activation of the Frontal Lobes is involved in God – Realization.

The experience of enlightenment, of non–separation, does not necessarily coincide with the experience of a living God–presence. In Sri Kalki's teaching more than the deactivation of the overactivity in the parietal lobes in necessary to move from enlightenment to God–realization. He speaks about the activation of the frontal lobes as a necessary neurological change for God to come alive in the consciousness of a person. The frontal lobes are associated with the individual will. Many mystical traditions speak about the merging of the individual will with the will of God as both a doorway to and result of God–realization.

This, however, cannot happen if the frontal lobes are underactive. It is a universal law that anything incomplete in nature seeks its own completion. My own findings in neurophysiology (which deviate from official, university-sanctioned science) show that the frontal lobes of practically all people are chronically underactive. This means they simply do not have enough neurotransmitters and electrical energy to function anywhere near optimum. On a subjective experience level, this is equal to a weakened self-will and an experience of dullness.

Boredom is only possible with underactive frontal lobes. Dopamine, the essential neurotransmitter for frontal lobe activity, is necessary for feelings of enchantment with life and bliss, often described to accompany mystical union with God. Lack of dopamine will increase the person's urge to maintain their self-will and not let it merge with a greater reality, because something is felt as yet incomplete on the individual level. It is like dying: a person, whose life feels complete and fulfilled usually has a much easier time to die when the time comes. A person who feels something is missing in life will often cling to life much more. If the deekshas have the effect of activating the frontal lobes, this could give completion to the individual will, its fullest flowering. At the full flowering of the individual will, it would naturally merge with the greater reality of God.

From this perspective, a "big ego" is actually nothing more than a compensation of a weak ego that seeks its own completion. But without full activation of the frontal lobes and dopamine saturation, the ego will never find its own completion and subsequent merger into God. To judge a big ego and fixation on one's individual will as lower consciousness, as is done so often in spiritual teachings, is useless, because a weak self–will has a natural urge to fixate on the individual, no matter what our conscious intentions may be. The solution can only come about with an actual change on the physiological level, which liberates the individual will from its struggle against surrendering into a greater reality.

3. **Sri Kalki says that enlightenment has to be given, it is a gift of Grace.**

In the past 15 years, Dr. Hartmut Müller from Germany developed a new paradigm of physics called Global Scaling. This exiting new expansion of quantum physics shows beyond doubt that consciousness is the most fundamental "substance" of the universe and that it contains an original design of everything in the universe, following an exact mathematical formula.

The distance between planets, stars and whole galaxies, the distance between electrons and nucleons in every atom, the optimum ph for human blood, all this and everything else in the material universe follows the same mathematical structure. This original design is such that everything operates on the least level of stress and the maximum level of efficiency at all times.

An atom is at all moments attuned to the source intelligence via a syntropic field. These syntropic fields allow an atom to always "know" how to function with the least amount of stress and maximum efficiency. Human beings seem to be the only manifested forms of creation that have to some degree lost their attunement to these syntropic fields of life and unity. Once this loss has produced some changes in the brain of the individual person, to re–attune oneself with the syntropic fields of unity is extremely difficult, because we do not know any longer what these fields are. We then create all kinds of mythologies, religions, scientific theories etc about life to fill the void.

A person with an overactive OAA in the parietal lobes and an underactive frontal lobe will seek enlightenment from the experience of separation. All spiritual striving and seeking is in some sense part of the problem, because it occurs as a reaction to the loss of attunement with the syntropic fields of unity. If our seeking is based in the problem, it is unlikely that it will end in the solution. If the attunement to the syntropic fields of unity can simply be given, it is indeed possible that enlightenment can happen for everyone.

The original design of the human brain is to perceive unity as the intrinsic reality of life. This original design is latent, but it needs a naturally functioning brain to be anchored in human consciousness. If the deekshas attune the brain of a person to the syntropic fields of optimum brain functioning, the individual consciousness would soon realize its seamlessness with unity.

4. **Sri Kalki says that enlightenment is a biological and genetic phenomenon.**

Traditional spirituality often assigns a very low status to the importance of the body. It is often seen as just a vessel for consciousness, a shirt that the soul is wearing. Modern physics shows that Sri Kalki's view is much more in alignment with what we know about the nature of matter. A distinct dividing line between matter, energy and spirit is illusory. Based on the brilliant vortex model of the atom that was formulated by Lord Kelvin in 1867, we can see that every atom has the size of the entire universe, and the material objects we perceive are only the densest aspects of atoms.

Matter is the result of an energetic continuum of vortexes of energy taking on increasing density. As Max Planck described in 1910, in this process of energy condensation, matter fluctuates billions of times per second between being matter and being a formless pre–material energy. From this perspective, it makes sense to assume that spiritual transformation has to be anchored on the physical level. When it reaches the densest level of manifestation, all other levels are automatically taken care of, because matter is not at all devoid of the higher dimensions of creation.

On the contrary, matter appears so dense, because it includes all the other levels. So when the material or biological level is enlightened, everything else is included. On the genetic level, it is interesting to note that human DNA is 173 centimeters long. Only 3 cm carry active genetic information. Modern biochemistry is puzzled at this seeming wastefulness of nature and calls the inactive parts of the DNA introns, useless waste material.

This is a very questionable assumption, as nature does not produce waste anywhere. The introns are in my opinion (again I deviate from official science) equal to the latent spiritual potential of the human being. It is my contention that the deekshas flood the inert parts of the DNA with photons, thus activating them. Photons are nature's bridge between subtle energy and matter. Photonresonance is the process by which information from the subtle realms is distributed from the DNA throughout the cell. The 3 cm of usually active DNA material carry information needed for mere survival, but when the rest of the DNA molecule becomes active (able to use photonresonance), we can move far beyond mere survival to awaken to our full potential.

5. Sri Kalki says that the Collective Mind or Ancient Mind determines our individual state of Mind.

In the 1950s, Dr. Hans Selye, endocrinologist of the University of Montreal, showed that the brain of every normal person is in a chronic state of survival stress that would only be appropriate in an acutely life threatening situation. This stress response is something we have adapted to so deeply that we do not perceive it anymore as particularly stressful. However, in this stress response state, we are bound to be highly conditioned by our environment and the collective unconscious.

Brain research shows that stress response patterns cause a dominance of high–frequency beta waves in the brain. While in beta, the brain is only capable of primitive stimulus–response patterns that we largely adopt from our environment and the collective human consciousness and real change is next to impossible. Beta is also the state of the least self–healing ability of the body. Spiritual practice can to some degree relax the stress response of the brain and allow more decelerated alpha, theta and delta waves.

However, research shows that individual spiritual practice is far less effective than a given attunement with syntropic fields of life and unity. At the *Tracker School* of Tom Brown Jr., the world's leading expert in wilderness skills, a neuro-scientist examined the effects of spending time in a pure wilderness. His findings where truly stunning: While it takes a novice usually well over a year of dedicated mediation practice to sustain an alpha state for a few hours, people who never meditated in their lives could sustain deep alpha for hours after only 48 hours in pure wilderness.

Since nature is attuned to syntropic fields of life, it will entrain the human brain to its own syntropic fields much faster than when an un–attuned brain seeks its attunement through effort. It is my contention that in individual practice, too much of the energy with which the seeker practices comes from the Ancient Mind of struggle and lack. Again, the search is based too much in the problem and not in the solution. This seems to be as close to a scientific validation for the need of grace as there can be.

Conclusion

Many scientists and spiritual leaders have called for a marriage of science and spirituality. After modern science was founded in the 17th century as a reaction to centuries of blind faith, for about two hundred years, scientists tried to confirm the objectivist–mechanistic world view of Descartes and Newton. This search finally merged into the staggering discoveries of quantum physics in the early 20th century, which showed that mystics had described reality quite accurately for millennia. What has been missing so far was a system of spiritual transformation that delivers scientific, precise and repeatable results. It is my contention, from scientific investigation, personal experience and anecdotal evidence, that the work of Sri Kalki is the first spiritual system to deliver such results, possibly on a global scale.

Appendix 3

The Dark Night of the Soul and Brainscience

A Scientific Commentary on the Transformation Process through Deeksha By Christian Opitz

(christian@powerorganics.com)

In 1977, Ilya Prigogine was awarded the Nobel Prize in theoretical chemistry for his discovery of dissipative structures. Prigogine described how every natural system grows in a non–linear way: the organizing structure of a system is at some point no longer useful and has to disintegrate before the new structure can emerge. A prime example of this principle is the transformation of a caterpillar into a butterfly. A caterpillar does not really become a butterfly in the cocoon. Rather, it turns into a chaotic molecular mesh. Out of this chaos, the structure of the butterfly spontaneously emerges.

Mystics have always been aware of this principle. The dissolution of the current sense of self and God before one can experience the true self and God is a common theme in the spiritual teachings of the ages. The medieval Christian mystic Meister Eckhart expressed this knowing in his famous prayer: "Lord, free me from you so that I can truly find you."

Christian mystics called this passage of losing oneself before finding absolute truth the Dark Night of the Soul. The term Dark Night does not necessarily refer to a horrible experience, rather the word Dark implies that one does not see anymore where one is going or how to get there. While every person and every deeksha is unique, this process seems to be a very common one for those who have received deeksha.

From a scientific point of view, the deeksha is a uniquely effective means of not only inducing the Dark Night experience, but more importantly, to actually make it fruitful. Many people experience some kind of crisis and loss of identity in their spiritual journey, but until now very few have emerged out of such experiences into full enlightenment. In my opinion, the deeksha process is the first ever means to make this transition possible for all of humanity. There are two primary factors that make the deeksha process far more effective than anything else to guide people through the Dark Night into full enlightenment:

1. The activation of the quiescence and arousal system.

Sri Kalki says that everything fully experienced turns into joy. There are two basic systems of awareness in the brain, the 'quiescence' and the 'arousal' system. When someone can experience something with a fully functional quiescence system, which means total awareness, the arousal system becomes activated and joy is experienced. Thus, Sri Kalki's statement is fully supported by neuro-scientific insight. This also matches the Taoist teaching that at their end points, yin and yang transform into each other.

However, the normal human brain does not have a functional quiescence system. We therefore tend to recoil from so many of our experiences in life because they do not become joyful. When the parietal lobes are chronically overactive, as I described in a recent article, the quiescence system of the brain is severely handicapped. Likewise, with the chronic underactivity in the frontal lobes, the arousal system of the brain is equally underactive. This leads to a biological urge to never fully experience anything, thus preventing the transformation of any experience into joy.

Without fully experiencing the inner sense of disorientation and chaos in the Dark Night phase, one cannot pass through it fully. The caterpillar does not resist its own dissolution and can therefore emerge as the butterfly out of its own destruction. Human consciousness however does resist these experiences as long as the brain is functioning the way that has been normal for human beings until now.

Biological urges are simply stronger than conscious intentions. Imagine someone told you that you get fully enlightened if you just don't sleep for six months. There goes your enlightenment. No matter how dedicated you are, the biological urge to sleep will be stronger. Therefore spiritual practices that are performed while the brain is stuck in the limited patterns of an underactive quiescence–arousal system can only give temporary states of enhanced awareness and joy, which for most people cannot lead to a dissolution of the old sense of self and the emergence of enlightenment.

If our brain is biologically wired to the pattern of not experiencing with full awareness, the best intentions to change this are quite powerless. However, a direct attunement tc the original design of the brain can effortlessly activate the natural functioning of the quiescence–arousal system. This is what the deekshas seem to cause very effectively. Then one can naturally surrender to whatever one's experience is, because there is a biological basis for such surrender.

To illustrate the difference in effectiveness between intention-based change and a biological change via direct attunement, let's take a look at strength. Strength is a neurological function, not a quality of muscles. The factors that limit a person's physical strength are neurological inhibitions. That's why a person during an epileptic seizure can have superhuman strength, because the neurological inhibitions fall away. These inhibitions affect other brain areas than the inhibitions that keep a person from being naturally enlightened, but otherwise they both are really the same process.

The world record for the bench press is 897 pounds. This is the result of an extremely talented athlete working very hard with all his desire and intention to be super strong. A gorilla shares 99% of the genetic makeup of a human being, yet without any intention or training or effort, the average gorilla has the strength that equal a 4000 pound bench press!

All a gorilla does is that he is attuned to his natural design. Gorillas don't try to be strong; they just are what they are. A human being disconnected from the original design can never match the natural strength that comes effortlessly to a gorilla. Since the biochemical process of neurological inhibition is the same, whether it's the inhibition of physical strength or of the quiescence–arousal system, this example can show us why the deeksha as a given attunement to our original brain design is so much more powerful than intention-based efforts.

2. The activation and regeneration of the septum pellucidum.

In the 1950s, neuroscientists discovered that the activation of the septum pellucidum, a brain center right in the middle of the brain, can instantly heal chronic pain, depression and anxiety, give a sense of deep peace, and above all, of joy. However, due to the neurological overactivity in the parietal lobes and the resulting lack of neurological energy for the rest of the brain, the septum pellucidum of almost everyone is chronically underactive.

This actually leads to a shrinking of the size of this important brain center, which in turn makes joy and aliveness less and less available to a person. This then activates a person's search for experiences that induce joy, because joy is natural and we are biologically wired to experience it. However, once the septum pellucidum has shrunk, only extreme stimulation can activate it to produce some joy.

This is the real biological base of addictions to drugs, overstimulation of the senses and all things of a rajasic or tamasic nature. The septum pellucidum is the brain's reward center and when it is not functioning naturally, we experience reward or joy mostly through unnatural means. Even in people who live a very pure lifestyle, the experience of joy is often dependent on conditions.

One of the most common descriptions of the enlightened state is that of unconditional joy. In other words, a truly enlightened person has a naturally functioning reward center which is always "on", not just under certain circumstances.

A naturally functioning septum pellucidum makes every experience of life rewarding, no matter what it is. As Sri Kalki says, everything fully experienced turns into joy. A healthy septum pellucidum allows us to experience joy in everything, making everything rewarding, including the experience of the Dark Night.

This makes it possible to actually go through such experiences of inner chaos without a biological urge trying to direct us away from them. For the last seven years, I have invented and investigated methods for activating the septum pellucidum. Looking at the brain changes in people who undergo the deeksha process, I have come to the conclusion that this is by far the most powerful means to activate and regenerate the septum pellucidum available today. This alone makes the deeksha process incredibly effective as a means for total inner transformation.

Conclusion:

From a scientific point of view, the deeksha process is unsurpassed in its effectiveness and logic, because it works according to the natural design of human beings. The old way of trying to transform oneself against the momentum of biological urges and programming that manifest the experience of separation and suffering was never based in natural principles, and has therefore only worked for few people. If enlightenment is our natural state, as so many mystics have said, then only a natural process will be effective in awakening humanity to it.

Our search for the solution to humanity's suffering must come from a different foundation than the reality of suffering.

Working against biological urges with intention–based effort is part of the reality of suffering, not part of its solution. Being given an attunement to our original design through Divine Grace is the way of nature, and all other life forms already participate in this natural way.

I am currently conducting further research into the effects of the deeksha process. This includes investigating factors that could perhaps make the human brain more receptive to the deeksha energy. It is an exciting new horizon for science that might finally bring science and spirituality together in a whole new way where both complement and support each other for the sake of humanity.

Glossary

Amma the name popularly used to refer to Bhagavan's wife, Sri Padmavati Devi. She is regarded as an incarnation of the Divine Mother, and is considered an Avatar, along with Bhagavan.

Ancient Mind rather than having separate individual minds, Bhagavan says that each of us is simply a channel for this collective, primeval mind, which has existed as a continually growing **morphogenetic field** since the beginning of human history. It includes all the human tendencies that we generally tend to identify with as ours – jealousies, anger, hurt, frustration, lust, happiness, greed, warring, and so on.

Antaryamin the Indwelling Presence, or **atman**, known in the West as **higher self**, **essence** or **inner divinity**. This becomes our identity once the illusion of a fixed and separate **self** is dissolved.

Ascension a state of full body enlightenment wherein the physical body merges with the so-called light body, a state that has been experienced by **ascended masters** such as Babaji, Ramalinga Swami, St. Germaine, and several others in the course of human history.

Assemblage point derived from the teachings of Don Juan, a Yaqui medicine man, it refers to various centers of consciousness in the physical/subtle bodies, which determine our experience of reality. The **deeksha** shifts our assemblage point so we can move into a permanent state of altered reality.

Atman our essential self, the divinity within. It is the individualized aspect of **Brahman**. See also **antaryamin**.

Avatar a descent of divinity into human form. Each avatar incarnates for a specialized purpose in order to raise humanity to the next level of collective evolution. Einstein was an avatar for physics; Bhagavan is an avatar for enlightenment. We are now entering the age of the **collective avatar**, says Bhagavan, and expects that this avataric consciousness will flow through a **'critical mass'** of people, who will then give enlightenment to the rest of the world as we transition into the Golden Age.

Bhagavan literally means 'bestower of blessings', and is a Hindu term referring to anyone who has realized God. It is also the current legal name of an avatar in south India whose only claim for himself is that he is a technician, whose specialty is being able to give enlightenment through a neurobiological reorganization of the brain.

Brahman the universal spirit that pervades all creation, and which exists beyond creation. When individualized through any point of creation, it is known as the **atman**.

Chakra literally wheel in Sanskrit. The **kundalini** energy flows through these 7 centers of energy along the spine, maintaining the life force of the body. When the chakras are dormant, one lives in separation consciousness. When they are fully activated, one becomes enlightened.

Consciousness Scale David Hawkins, author of the book, *Power vs. Force*, uses a system known as applied kinesiology to devise a scale of consciousness ranging from 0 to 1000. At the bottom of the scale are states of mind such as guilt, shame and fear, while the upper end of the scale reflects love, joy, and various levels of enlightenment. He says, interestingly, that when a person vibrates on the higher end of this scale, he or she can offset millions of people vibrating at the lower ends of the scale, an assertion which explains how mass enlightenment might eventually be accomplished.

Critical mass a certain amount, when achieved, at which transformation suddenly and irreversibly happens. This could relate to water turning to steam, or to the **hundredth monkey phenomenon**, or to global enlightenment!

Dark night of the Soul (or Cloud of Unknowing) a period of time, sometime after enlightenment has taken place, when the personal unconscious is emptied out. It can be experienced as an intense dryness, emptiness, and inner struggle, similar to what Jesus experienced in the wilderness before the start of his ministry. This process of clearing the unconscious can only happen once the self has dissolved, and is not the same, in Bhagavan's definition, as the periodic slumps that we pass through before enlightenment.

Darshan a Sanskrit word meaning interview or gathering.

Dasaji the former name used for the **guides** at Oneness University. The term literally means, 'one who serves', and refers to both male and female disciples.

Deeksha the transfer of energy, directed by Bhagavan, which creates a neurobiological shift in the brain, ultimately leading to enlightenment. Although usually a hands-on experience, the transfer can also take place through a glance, prayer, or thought, or by simply being in the presence of someone who is enlightened.

Dimensions also known as **lokas**, these are a multitude of worlds, each operating on a different vibrational frequency, within the created universes. The physical world is only of these. Bhagavan speaks of 21 lokas, each associated with a specific chakra, (7 within the body, 7 below the body, and 7 above the body), which incarnated humans are allowed to explore.

Dosha the ayurvedic system of Indian medicine proposes that the health of the human body has to do with the balancing of three doshas – vata, pitta, and kapha. When these doshas are in balance, the body becomes more receptive to the **deeksha**.

Ego the Western equivalent to what Hindus identify as the **self**.

Enlightenment a state of consciousness where the **self**, or **ego**, is recognized to be an illusion. When the self dissolves, a new identity emerges, which is the **antaryamin**, or **higher self**. Bhagavan maintains that enlightenment is a neurobiological phenomenon. It cannot be achieved through ones own efforts, any more than a drowning man can pull himself out by his own hair. Rather, it can be given as a gift of grace through a transfer of energy known as the **deeksha**, which reorganizes the brain leading to enlightenment. The first stage of enlightenment is the witness state, which in later stages deepens into states of unity consciousness with all creation, and eventually with God – I Am That. As more and more people become enlightened, says Bhagavan, it will create a **morphogenetic field** which will ultimately result in a collective enlightenment for all humanity.

Essence see **antaryamin**

Golden Age Bhagavan speaks repeatedly of this as an Age of Enlightenment. Also called the Satya Yuga, or Age of Truth, he says that according to many Hindu scholars, this officially began in 2003, although it may take a few decades for the effects to be fully manifest. The Golden Age is expected to last 1000 years.

Guides the teachers, helpers, or deeksha-givers at Oneness University. Formerly known as **dasajis**, they had been through years of specialized training with Bhagavan before the public deeksha programs began.

Higher self see **antaryamin**

Hundredth monkey theory a metaphor for the way **morphogenetic fields** function, the story goes that a certain tribe of monkeys were observed on a Japanese island learning to wash sweet potatoes in the river before eating them. As more and more monkeys began to teach each other to do this, something very unexpected happened. Suddenly, one day, as a hypothetical hundredth monkey learned this new behavior, it was discovered that every single monkey on the island began to wash their sweet potatoes in the river, and not only that, but every monkey of that species on neighboring islands also began washing their sweet potatoes. A critical mass had been reached in the evolution of that species, which affected the mass consciousness fields of that species, creating an entirely new genetic pathway!

Inner Divinity see **antaryamin**

Kali Yuga Hindu cosmology speaks of 4 **yugas**, or 'ages', which follow each other in linear succession. The darkest of these is the Kali Yuga, and the lightest of these is the **Satya Yuga**. We are currently in a transition from a Kali Yuga to a Satya Yuga.

Kalki in Hindu mythology, the tenth incarnation of Vishnu, who is predicted to come at the end of the **Kali Yuga** to lead humanity into the **Golden Age**. It is the name formerly applied to **Bhagavan**, until he decided to stop using it due to the controversy it was creating. This is the age of the collective avatar, he maintains, and everybody who is enlightened, and working for the enlightenment of humanity, is a 'kalki'.

Karma the law of universal action which states that we reap according to what we sow. It is the means whereby a soul gathers experience through its journey of existence.

Kosha literally means body or sheath. There are 5 koshas that interpenetrate each other in every incarnated human being – the **anandamayakosha**, or bliss body, the **vignanamayakosha**, or wisdom body, the **manamayakosha**, or mind body, the **pranamayakosha**, or etheric body, and finally, the **annamayakosha**, or food body, which our senses recognize as the physical body.

Kundalini the life force energy that runs through channels, or **nadis** in the spine known as the ida, pingala, and sushumna. It passes through 7 **chakras**, or centers, in the body as it rises from its dormant position at the bottom of the spine up to the crown of the head, where it meets the descending cosmic energies activated by the **deeksha**, resulting in **enlightenment**.

Loka a location in space and time existing separately and independently of the physical dimension. Many people, as they go through peak states following their enlightenment, find themselves able to travel in and out of these lokas. A shaman is one who has learned to travel through these lokas at will. See also **dimension**.

Morphogenetic fields literally form generating fields, these fields are hypothesized by British biologist Rupert Sheldrake, to exist as a genetic blueprint for every species on Earth. They permeate the **thoughtsphere** of any given species, and determine every aspect of its evolution. As illustrated by the **hundredth monkey phenomenon**, a quantum leap in evolution takes place whenever a critical mass within that species has learned a new behavior or achieved a new state of consciousness.

Mukti literally means freedom in Sanskrit, and refers to the freedom from suffering which results from enlightenment.

Nadi the channels in the spine, and also throughout the body, which carry the **kundalini** energy.

Nagual a term used by the Yaqui shaman, Don Juan, to denote the realms of unified consciousness. The laws of the universe operate differently in this realm than in the physical realm.

Oneness University Bhagavan's training program in south India where various programs are offered to the public, including courses in parenting, emotional healing, ayurvedic cleansing, and enlightenment.

Phala Deeksha a specialized deeksha offered at Oneness University which puts participants into a state where they are able to experience and interact with Amma and Bhagavan in their cosmic body. They are then invited to ask for what they desire, whether it is in the realm of health, enlightenment, finances, relationships, or other issues.

Sadhana a Sanskrit term meaning spiritual practice

Samadhi refers to states of unity consciousness. Classically, there are 4 stages of samadhi in Hindu mysticism. **Savikalpa samadhi** refers to the early peak experiences of oneness with God. As one spends more time in this state, it evolves into **nirvikalpa samadhi**, a relatively non-functional state where the person is permanently anchored in oneness. In the 3rd stage, **sahaj samadhi**, the physical body becomes attuned to this oneness to the extent that one is now able to function normally while also holding unity-consciousness. In the 4th stage of **soruba samadhi**, which is relatively rare, the entire physical body dissolves into light. This process is also known as **ascension**, and one who has achieved this state is known as an **ascended master**.

Satya Yuga in Hindu cosmology, this is the lightest of four yugas, or 'ages', which follow each other in linear succession. We are currently transitioning from a **Kali Yuga** to a Satya Yuga, which can also be referred to as a **Golden Age**.

Self the Hindu equivalent to the term **ego**, referring to an illusory center of identity which is based in the concept of separation, of existence apart from the whole.

Soul also known as **atman, higher self, antaryamin** or **essence**, it is a center of identity based in unity consciousness. It is a flow of consciousness revealed as the basis of human identity once the illusory self is dissolved.

Srimurti Picture of Amma and Bhagawan, often felt to have some kind of divine presence in itself.

Supramental consciousness, or **supermind** a **morphogenetic field** of unity consciousness, as expounded by Sri Aurobindo and the Mother, which was anchored into human collective consciousness in 1956, and will be further activated within each human being in the course of humanity's journey of spiritual evolution.

Thoughtsphere the sum total of all the thoughts and emotions held within the **Ancient Mind** of humanity. This will dissolve once mass enlightenment takes place, to be replaced by the **supermind,** an enlightened field of consciousness that will permeate the **morphogenetic fields** of every species on Earth!

Zero point a term coined by geologist Gregg Braden, it refers to the convergence of two long term geological trends, one being the gradual deterioration of Earths electromagnetic fields, the other being the steady increase in her base harmonic frequency. Braden expects that there will be a collective initiation of the planet when this moment arrives.

End Note

Worldwide Deeksha Contacts

For those who may wish to make a personal pilgrimage to Oneness University, please go to my website, www.kiarawindrider.com for schedules and information, as well as articles and links on this and related themes. There are a number of other excellent websites you may also wish to browse through, including **www.livinginjoy.com**, **www.globaloneness.com**, and **www.trueawakening.org**. There are currently several courses being offered for those who are seeking enlightenment as well as programs for those who wish to go deeper and be trained as deeksha-givers.

There is a growing network of people around the world who have been empowered to give the deeksha themselves, who are listed on the above websites. You may wish to contact the person closest to your area if you wish to experience the power of the deeksha for yourself. Since the avataric consciousness knows no boundaries of time, space, or religion, you may also begin to connect with Amma or Bhagavan within your own heart.

The official Golden Age Foundation website, www.onenessuniversity.org was inaugurated on March 7, 2005, and will be continually updated with relevant articles, course information and global contacts for receiving deekshas and courses.

About Kiara Windrider

Kiara Windrider, MA, is a licensed psychotherapist, spiritual teacher, and author of *Doorway to Eternity: A Guide to Planetary Ascension.* Born and raised in India, he spent 22 years studying and practicing in the US before heeding an inner call to return to India, where he first met Bhagavan in August 2003. He met his wife, Grace, shortly before his return to India.

They have both undergone the enlightenment process, including the empowerment to give 'deeksha', and are both committed to doing all they can to facilitate humanity's entry into the Golden Age. Kiara and Grace are available to give deekshas, workshops, and lectures worldwide on the themes of planetary healing and enlightenment.

Feedback and comments are welcome. Kiara can be reached at **kiara@doorwaytoeternity.com,** or through his website, **www.kiarawindrider.com.**

